The Doctrine of Christ: Essential Truth of Scripture

Chris A. Legebow

ISBN-13: 978-1-988914-01-5

DEDICATION

I thank God for the excellent Bible classes and Christian training I received
at my churches I have been a part of in Canada and the USA as they
helped to develop me in the truths of Christ.
I thank God for those saints who imparted into me the truths they had
been taught and who layed hands on me praying an impartation blessing.   I
thank God for Christian Media especially
Trinity Broadcasting Network and the Gloy Star Satellite system
for connecting me with excellent training and teaching .

Chris A. Legebow

CONTENTS

ACKNOWLEDGMENTS

All Scripture taken from Bible Gateway.com

Modern English version (MEV)
.

1 INTRODUCTION

Chapter 1

The essential doctrines of Christ are explained in this book. What it exactly means is that these are the key values of the Christian faith as expressed through the Scriptures. Particularly mentioned by the Apostle Paul, who founded many churches and wrote most of our New Testament, these truths were passed on from church to church and recorded in scripture. they include the following truths:

Hebrews 6: 1 Therefore, leaving the elementary principles of the doctrine of Christ, let us go on to maturity, not laying again a foundation of repentance from dead works and of faith toward God, 2 of instruction about washings, the laying on of hands, the resurrection of the dead, and eternal judgment. 3 This we will do if God permits.

The core foundation stones include Repentance, Faith toward God, Baptisms, The Resurrection of the Dead and Eternal Judgement. They are the main parts of this book. I have also included the Apostle's Creed. The Apostle's Creed is not scripture, but it summarizes the truths of scriptures that Jesus and the Apostles taught. Christians learned, memorized and taught others the core values of the Christian faith by reciting the Creed together for hundreds of years. Most people did not have direct access to the New Testament letters of the disciples until much later. They memorized the truths and taught them to others.

It is my hope that you will be encouraged in your Christian faith and that you may use these truths, to teach others about the Christian faith

2 THE APOSTLES CREED

Chapter 2

This teaching is an introduction to the Christian faith – what all Christians believe. A Creed is what people believe. It is a summary of their beliefs or core values. The Christian Church started as Jesus rose from the dead and appeared to his disciples. They were not yet called Christians until the Apostle Paul's day at Antioch. For over 300 years the Christians were persecuted by Rome. Roman Emperors believed they themselves were gods and killed anyone who didn't worship them.

In 325 A.D., the Roman Emperor Constantine converted to Christianity and made it possible for Christians to worship with freedom. Because of the council of Nicaea in 325, the Apostles Creed was formed and the spread of Christianity was strong (Wikipedia). The first Church approved by Rome was called The Roman Catholic Church. God's miracle of completely turning around a perverted pagan nation to repent and turn to the truths of Christ is beyond human explanation. God used the Roman Empire to spread Christianity because of the Roman roads that paved all of the Empire. They were excellent architects and builders and had paved roads throughout the Empire. This made it easy for Christianity to spread. Also, Latin was the common language throughout the Empire. It made it possible for all people to know the good news of salivation in all different countries. It was spoken and preached but also translated from scripture.

Please know that the meaning of catholic in the Creed was termed as universal. I am not a Roman Catholic but I am a Christian Catholic – meaning that I believe in One True Church of Jesus Christ in the earth and in heaven – even though there be many denominations there is one true Church who believe in the core trues listed in the Creed; some are protestants and some are modern day Roman Catholics. I am a protestant in faith – believing in one universal Church. The Creed that was agreed upon first was known as the Nicaean Creed and later known as the Apostle's Creed. They recorded what they believed were the key aspects of the Christian Faith.

If you truly believe these things in the Creed, you are a Christian. If you do not believe all the things in this Creed, you are not a Christian. That final decision was determined in 390 A. D.

Unfortunately, not everyone teaches or preaches these simple truths from the pulpit. The main denominational churches still teach the Creed and say it together regularly. Some Pentecostal and Charismatic Churches do not openly speak these things from the pulpit or in services. Please know these are core values shared by all Christians. Their origin is in scripture, but you will not find a scripture that lists the Apostle's Creed. Clearly it is a way for humans to organize our beliefs in God through Jesus Christ.

The Apostles Creed

1. I believe in God,
the Father almighty,
Creator of heaven and earth,
2. I believe in Jesus Christ, his only Son, our Lord.
3. He was conceived by the power of the Holy Spirit and born of the Virgin Mary.
4. Under Pontius Pilate, He was crucified, died, and was buried.
5. He descended to the dead. On the third day he rose again.
6. He ascended into heaven and is seated at the right hand of the Father.
7. He will come again to judge the living and the dead.
8. I believe in the Holy Spirit,
9. the holy catholic(universal) Church, the communion of saints,
   the communion of saints,
10. the forgiveness of sins,
11. the resurrection of the body,
12. and the life everlasting.
Amen.

Explanation of the Creed

SECTION 1
Almighty God (the Father) who is known in the King James Version Bible as LORD – that comes from the tetragrammaton YHVH - we pronounce it with vowels Jehovah. He is almighty God, the God of Israel. He is the God who created all things and created Adam and Eve. He revealed Himself to Noah and to Abraham and Moses. There are many aspects to Him as God. He is reveals Himself in many ways throughout the Bible. I include the following list of revelations of God from a chapter from my book on Kinds of Prayer.

LORD – I AM that IAM – Jehovah

Our God is a personal God not some unknown entity.

God is as close or more close and intimate than a parent. He is the source of our life, our planet etc. He chooses to reveal Himself as a personal friend. God cares for us and calls us His people and His children.

Rapha – The LORD our Healer – If you know that He is Jehovah the Healer, you know certainly He is not going to make you ill. It would go against His very nature.

Tsidkenu Jeremiah 23: 6 – The LORD our righteousness. Please understand that God called Himself our righteousness even before He revealed Himself as Jesus our Saviour. Salvation was the plan for us all along. God was making covenant with people and revealing Himself as our righteousness thousands of years before Jesus died on the cross. We could never be righteous or pure or Holy without God. He is our righteousness.

Leviticus 20: 7-8 Jehovah Kaddish the one who sanctifies us or sets us apart. In the New Testament we are called the Church which is the Greek Word Ecclesia which means called out ones" out of the world and into the kingdom of God. We are separate because of our God.
We are people called out of darkness into His light. 1 Corinthians 1: 30 tells us this.

Judges 6: 24 Jehovah Shalom - He is the God of our peace. I have always thought this simply means peace. In recent years I have heard teaching that the Hebrew word literally means wholeness or completeness – nothing missing, nothing broken, oneness, perfection. The Peace that God brings surpasses anything on earth.

If we live according to the media reports or people's news or live according to our feelings, we will live an up and down life. Our peace is in the LORD. He can calm us and give us peace in any situation. Our God lives in our hearts – I'm not talking about the physical organ. I am talking about the inner most chamber of your being – the core of you – the living soul. You are a spirit, you have a soul (mind, will and emotions) and you live in your physical body – the one God gave you. Our God lives in us. He brings us peace.

In the midst of any situation, you can have peace because He is the peace maker. He manifests His peace with His presence.

Jehovah Shamma – Omnipresent – He is always present. He is

everywhere. He is with me here. He is with me no matter where I go. He is with believers in other parts of the earth – all over the earth – living in us – simultaneously omnipresent. Ezekiel 48: 35 and Hebrews 13: 5.

Jehovah Rapha – the Healer Exodus 15 and 26 and Psalm 103: 3 Bless the LORD who heals all my diseases. If you don't have the faith to know that God is your healer, pray the scripture for yourself. I will talk about it in a different chapter but as we pray God\s word, it releases faith in us and it brings us into alignment with God's Word. Remember His Word is His will.

Just as much as you believe He forgives all your sins, you should believe He is your healer. The blood of Jesus cleanses our sin, heals us and delivers us.
Isaiah 53 reveals our Saviour and Healer.

Isaiah 53: 5
But he was wounded for our transgressions,
he was bruised for our iniquities;
the chastisement of our peace was upon him,
and by his stripes we are healed.

If you do not know He is your healer, literally pray the scripture for yourself or the person who needs healing. I mean literally say the words to God saying " LORD you said that by your stripes we are healed. I pray for healing for…" God's Word releases faith in the believer. The more you confess and pray the scriptures, the more your faith will grow.

I learned this years ago. I knew the Lord and had studied about God quite a bit, but no one had ever taught me to pray the scriptures. I believed I knew how to pray but it was only the starting point of my Christian life. I believed I knew God pretty well. But what happened was something horrible. Somebody I cared about very much was at the point of death. It was my pastor. We used to have a prayer chain in that church and they phoned to tell me that my pastor was deathly ill.

People may react differently but my reaction was horror and prayer. I had never had this type of need before someone literally in a life or death situation. By the next day, I had prayed everything I knew how to pray. I prayed in English and prayed in tongues (that is a Godly language that God Himself gives you to use). I knew it wasn't enough. What I did is I started searching through my concordance on every scripture that had to do with healing. I believe God quickened it to me. I knew I needed ammunition from God's Word. I started proclaiming those scriptures over my pastor. I started praying God's word Knowing that God is the same yesterday, today and forever. I would pray "God you healed the woman with the issue of blood, you can heal my pastor…" I personalized it totally and gave me a whole new realm of prayer – praying scriptures over my pastor.

I wish I could tell you it was a onetime event but it wasn't. It was an assignment from God because I knew I had to do it. I knew it wasn't God's will for him to die. He was in the prime of life, had a church, kids and grandchildren. He had much word in him to share and I knew in my spirit it was not his time to die. I knew that he was under attack for his life. It was a process of 2 years. The doctors had given him a negative report saying he would not live or if he did live he could be a vegetable. They said he might not be able to walk or preach again. I want to say I am one of the people God gave the assignment to. There were a core of us who gathered every day until he was completely healed. At first the church was so crowded there was barely room to get a seat. Other Pastors of other churches came to pray for him. People loved him. But there were a core of us who continued and continued, not accepting any negative report but believing in God's Word for complete healing for him.

This engaging in prayer and praying through a situation was once called "praying through" a situation. The Latter rain movement is my history as I come from a Church birthed before it and famous for it. During WW II, people would go to the church every day praying for the safety of their loved ones and of our troops.

Jehovah Rohi is Jehovah our shepherd. He leads me. Psalm 23. He leads me beside living waters. He leads me into green pastures. He is a God who loves me and cares for my soul. God can lead you and direct you. I don't mean in a vague way. I mean He can direct you the right way and you will feel peace. I heard Gloria Copeland say this actually and it was "Let peace be your umpire". I like baseball so I understand the Umpire makes calls such as in or out or safe etc. The Holy Spirit is our Umpire. Gloria literally said if you are trying to make a decision but don't know the way – literally say to the Holy Spirit " Holy Spirit I believe I am going to go in this direction… state the way you believe might be best.. and say – if its not the best way please correct me." Literally the Holy Spirit will either check you in your spirit or release you. O that has been so important to me in many decisions. The Holy Spirit will always correct us if we obey His prompting.

I am talking about major decision making such as should I marry this person? Should I take this job? Should I move? I'm not talking about praying over what brand of cereal you are going to buy. For the most part I make all my own decisions. I have education and experience. I believe God lets me choose what I want. I am talking about times we are not sure – which way to go. It usually involves other people; it is usually complex. God will let us choose but if you are not sure – that should be brought to God in the manner I've described. God will lead you with His peace. If you feel a check in your spirit, you should not proceed. Obey the promptings of the Holy Spirit. I've learned this by testimony but also by experience.

God was so merciful to me. I was watching a TV show I had always watched but I felt a check like "don't watch this. It is no good for you. It's not right turn it off." I had never had an issue with this show in the past. It was something I always watched. Be obedient to the LORD to obey those promptings. Later, I was begging God to have mercy on me and forgive me because of the way my spirit felt – like garbage had been dumped in there – unclean. Should you get a prompting from the Holy Spirit that says that is not the direction for you – you get that feeling? You obey. It could be the purchase of a car, or marrying a person or going to a place. Be sensitive to let the Holy Spirit be your Peace Umpire.

I am not mentioning names for no reason. These people have impacted my life so tremendously that it has strengthened my Christian faith in the foundations of my being. If you hear names and you don't know who these people are, start searching the Internet and get some of their teachings. It will build your faith; it will teach you; you can learn things from mature saints who learned them from other faithful people. You don't have to learn the hard way – you can learn from others. You want spiritual help? You want to grow spiritually? These people I am mentioning will help you. That is why I am mentioning them, They don't pay me to mention names and I don't do it lightly. These people are proven ministers of God who live lives of integrity.

God knows you more than you know you. He knows you because He formed you and placed you in your mother's womb. He knows your character; He knows what will make you glad; He knows what you like because He created you to be that way.

Jehovah Jireh: Our Provider Genesis 22: 14

We thank Him for our daily bread; we should. He provides for us. I am not being religious; 2/3 of the people on earth do not have the luxury or quantity of things that we have in North America and Europe. We should thank God for supplying for us. I have never known hunger except on a fast. I know what it is like to go without food on purpose and feel hunger. There are people – even Christians in different countries who have known hunger and believe me they are thankful for their food. We should thank God for what we have. Food, clothing, shelter, freedom of worship… I could go on and on about the blessings we in North America have been give. Keep in an attitude of gratitude. It will make it easy for you to get into prayer without ceasing.

Be thankful for the small things as well as the big things. God cared enough about me that He cared if I had the cup of coffee I wanted. We should thank God for new things. Thanksgiving releases joy in your spirit and it releases blessings over your life. I want to always be thankful for what God has given me; I want to be in a posture of thanksgiving.

There is a Matisse painting of the Giver – it a picture of one hand clearly giving a bouquet of Beautiful coloured flowers to a second hand. That's God. He gives to us always, always, always. The fact you have air in your lungs or you can walk or run or do something, is God's gift to us. In the present, God is giving you life right this moment. Don't take it for granted; thank God for the small things. Thank God for the sunset being pretty. Cultivate a heart of thanksgiving, that you would be quick to be thankful.

Jehovah Jireh supplies our needs, but it isn't only financial. Oh yes it is financial. I could share with you story after story of how He has supplied for me financially, making a way for me, putting people in my life who gave to me etc. But it is more than just financial. He provides for us food, shelter, friends, family, opportunities. Use it financially. God wants to prosper you. In the Old Covenant the book of Deuteronomy is dedicated to teaching the blessings of the LORD towards His people – with things. Jesus is the Messiah who has fulfilled all of the requirements of the Old Covenant. We are partakers of the blessings. Jesus, the new Adam grafts us into His side. Jesus makes us heirs with Israel to bless us with all things we should have need of. Read the blessings of Deuteronomy 28 over yourself. Pray them for yourself if you haven't already done so. He supplies for us in all areas of need.

He comforts us with a comfort that goes beyond anything of this earth. Upon the loss of my mother, God comforted me so much. I was so close to my mother. Once she became a born-again spirit filled Christian, she and I became the closest friends sharing the things of God together, praying together, reading the Bible together etc. I am so comforted knowing she is with the LORD. I am so thankful for the memories of her praying and praising and taking communion with me. God comforts me knowing she is with Him. God can supply you with comfort that surpasses all of earthly knowledge upon the loss of a loved one.

You might know that your loved one knew the LORD but it can comfort you this way. The mercy God showed towards you in drawing you to Himself and saving you from yourself and from destruction – that same mercy was reaching out to your loved one. If you were praying for them and others were, you know God was releasing chances for those people to come to Christ. They had up to the last second of their life on earth to make a decision for Christ. Let God's mercy be a comfort to you.

Jehovah Nissi – the LORD our banner –
Ex 17: 15 Then Moses built an altar and called the name of it, The LORD Is My Banner;

He is our deliverer; He is our victory. I know what it is like to be in bondage. I don't just mean before I was saved. Even when I was first a Christian I had some things that were bondages. We don't use that language too much anymore. We kind of cleaned up the language and say they were bad habits. Bondage is like what the slave traders do. They still exist. I don't know if you know it or not. They place iron shackles on the wrists and ankles of the slaves. Those people are lead and they have no choice about what they are doing or where they are going. They are in irons, lead by an enemy, used and abused. They can't escape because of their bondages – those chains stop them from living a free life.

They are sins you can't seem to get away from. They always tempt you and you fail repeatedly. I've known people who have quit smoking and kept going back to it; people who were in bondage to alcohol or drugs and kept going back to it. They are weaknesses, bad habits, sins. They are bondages; they have a hold of you just as sure as those irons have hold of the human slaves, these sins have a hold of you. You can't get free on your own. Jehovah Nissi is our banner. He gives us victory. We used to sing a chorus " The Lion of Judah will break every chain and give to us the victory again and again." Do you know the Lion of Judah? He will break every chain. Just as sure as those iron chains can be broken with the right tools, Jesus can break those chains off you. This is what I mean. You wouldn't have to go to your 7 step programs any more.

Please know I am not against 7 step programs. Every alcoholic and drug addict they help is a tremendous thing. What I am telling you is that you can be set free spiritually so that do not need any support – it will be as though it never existed. You won't want it. You won't be tempted by it. You won't even consider it. You will be fixed on Jesus and the freedom that He has given you to do whatever you want with your life.

Jehovah Adoni – He is our master. Let's never get away from the idea that God is our Master – our teacher. Ex 21: 6 There is a teaching in the Old testament that talks about if you have a slave and in the 7th year that you set him free – he loves you and chooses to serve you, you are to take an awl and pierce through his ear. This shows he freely chooses to serve you for the rest of his life. Some masters were good to their slaves and gave them food, shelter, money etc. If you haven't done so, please read the Old Testament of how you were supposed to treat the slaves.
In the 7th year you had to set the slaves free, but some loved their masters so much they stayed by their own free will.

I made that decision when I was first a Christian. I realized Jesus had set me free. I had freedom to choose whatever I wanted. I had a new sense of freedom. IN fact I knew I didn't have to stay with the LORD. I could go and do anything – I could choose whatever life I wanted. I realized I had freedom. It was the first time in my life I felt free to do whatever I wanted. I said to the LORD I have seen you are good. You have given me freedom; its your way I want to do. I chose Him for all my life. I got my ears pierced. I often think of it in connection with that scripture – not always but often. It's a reminder to me that even though I am free – I am choosing my God – moment by moment day after day for the rest of my life. I willingly choose to serve the LORD. I am a willing servant of the LORD God Almighty; I choose to serve Him. I want to; it's my pleasure to do it.

God is my friend – the Holy Spirit my closest friend. I also remember God's majesty; He is sitting on a throne in heaven. Angels cover their faces because of the radiance of the glory that is on Him. Hosts of thousands of angels and saints are worshipping Him; He is LORD God almighty. Read chapter 7 Revelation about the glory of the LORD. There are thunders, lightning around the throne. Don't forget the grandeur of God. He has given you entrance by His blood into the Holy of Holies.

El Elyon – Psalm 91:1 He is the almighty, most high God. He is omnipotent. He lead Israel out of Egypt and literally divided the Red Sea so Israel could pass by on dry ground. He is a God of miracles and might.

El Shaddai – This is the last one I'll mention here. Gen 49: 25. He is all sufficient. He supplies more than what we need. Some religions have some gods who are higher than others. It is illogical to me. If there are some higher ones, why not just serve the higher ones? Why bother with the lower ones? There is no higher God than Jehovah – He is the LORD of LORDS and King and Kings. There are no other real gods. Demons fool people into worshipping them. They were angels who sinned with the Devil. They were thrown out of heaven. They live in the atmospheres of the earth. People make idols to worship these false gods – believing the lie they are gods. We are forbidden to make idols.

Don't pray to a picture of Jesus or a statue of Jesus – we are commanded to worship only the LORD. There is no idol. Don't worship the cross. It was the way Jesus died but in itself it is not Holy or special. Jesus is the one we should be worshipping. Don't pray to your prayer beads – they are simply beads. If they help you to remember to pray good – but in themselves they are nothing but beads. Most Protestants may not agree with me. I'm not against using things to help us to pray, but if you worship those things themselves, it is wrong. If you are using prayer beads to pray and reading this book, ask the LORD out loud " Lord can I continue to use these beads or am I using them in some sort of idolatry." Literally I believe God will speak to you. If He corrects you, obey Him. I once had a friend who was convicted by God for praying to pictures of Jesus. They were nice pictures of Jesus but God convicted her and said don't pray to images. No one really knows what Jesus looks like. The closest thing we have is the Shroud of Turin if it is authentic. We are forbidden by the 2nd commandment not to make idols or pray to them. We pray to God Himself – we don't need a picture.

Section 2
I believe in Jesus Christ, his only Son, our Lord.

Jesus – Jesus our Saviour – be thankful He is your Saviour who saved you from sin, death and hell. He is mighty to save. This section means you believe that Jesus Christ is the only Son of God. He was with God in the beginning; He is eternal. He will live forever. He is God. These next sections deal with the literal belief in these things as true. They are no analogies. They are not comparisons; they are truth.

John 1: 1 In the beginning was the Word, and the Word was with God, and the Word was God. 2 He was in the beginning with God. 3 All things were created through Him, and without Him nothing was created that was created. 4 In Him was life, and the life was the light of mankind. 5 The light shines in darkness, but the darkness has not overcome it.

Section 3
3. He was conceived by the power of the Holy Spirit and born of the Virgin Mary.

Christians believe that God chose the Virgin Mary to be the mother of Jesus. First of all, she was a Virgin. She was to be married to Joseph but became pregnant by God. It only happened once. It is humanly impossible for a virgin to give birth, but Christians believe God's Spirit came upon Mary and placed the seed of His Son Jesus in her womb. The angel greeted her with the good news and she willingly agreed to it. She came into agreement with God – God did not force her – she said " Let it be unto me". She knew it was an angel of God. She accepted something that could make her an outcast in her society.

Luke 1: 26 In the sixth month the angel Gabriel was sent from God to a city of Galilee named Nazareth, 27 to a virgin betrothed to a man whose name was Joseph, of the house of David. And the virgin's name was Mary. 28 The angel came to her and said, "Greetings, you who are highly favored. The Lord is with you. Blessed are you among women."

29 When she saw him, she was troubled by his words, and considered in her mind what kind of greeting this might be. 30 But the angel said to her, "Do not be afraid, Mary, for you have found favor with God. 31 Listen, you will conceive in your womb and bear a Son and shall call His name JESUS. 32 He will be great, and will be called the Son of the Highest. And the Lord God will give Him the throne of His father David, 33 and He will reign over the house of Jacob forever. And of His kingdom there will be no end."

34 Then Mary said to the angel, "How can this be, since I do not know a man?"

35 The angel answered her, "The Holy Spirit will come upon you, and the power of the Highest will overshadow you. Therefore the Holy One who will be born will be called the Son of God. 36 Listen, your cousin Elizabeth has also conceived a son in her old age. And this is the sixth month with her who was declared barren. 37 For with God nothing will be impossible."

38 Mary said, "I am the servant of the Lord. May it be unto me according to your word." Then the angel departed from her.

She could have rejected these words from the Angel. She did not. In her society to be pregnant outside of marriage meant certain death by stoning. It was a serious sin. Her husband to be, Joseph, was willing to show kindness to her by sending her away. He did not believe her story. He was going to cancel the wedding, until an angel appeared to him in a dream.

Joseph

Matthew 1: 18 Now the birth of Jesus Christ happened this way: After His mother Mary was engaged to Joseph, before they came together, she was found with child by the Holy Spirit. 19 Then Joseph her husband, being a just man and not willing to make her a public example, had in mind to send her away privately.

20 But while he thought on these things, the angel of the Lord appeared to him in a dream saying, "Joseph, son of David, do not be afraid to take Mary as your wife, for He who is conceived in her is of the Holy Spirit. 21 She will bear a Son, and you shall call His name JESUS, for He will save His people from their sins."

22 Now all this occurred to fulfill what the Lord had spoken through the prophet, saying, 23 "A virgin shall be with child, and will bear a Son, and they shall call His name Immanuel,"[a] which is interpreted, "God with us."

24 Then Joseph, being awakened from sleep, did as the angel of the Lord had commanded him, and remained with his wife, 25 and did not know her until she had given birth to her firstborn Son. And he called His name JESUS.

God confirmed the Virgin birth to Joseph; the truth was so real to him, he changed his plans and married her, which would have made him look poorly in the sight of the people. Everyone would have assumed that he was the child's father; sex outside of marriage, was punishable by death of both him and her. Although Joseph raised Jesus as his own son, Jesus had no human father.

Section 4
4. Under Pontius Pilate, He was crucified, died, and was buried.

We don't know much about Jesus as he was raised by Mary and Joseph except that they were believers in God and celebrated the feasts commanded by Moses. At 12 years old, Jesus wanders away from them and is later found teaching in the Temple at Jerusalem. What this means is Jesus had a sense of destiny from his youth onward. He was trained by Joseph to be a carpenter. At the age of 30, he began his ministry of teaching and preaching.

Here is the Apostle Paul's short version of the three year ministry of Jesus. Jesus preached in synagogues and in the Temple. He gathered 12 Apostles to himself to teach and disciple. He preached the good news of the coming of God's kingdom. He healed people; he raised the dead; he did mighty miracles. The Pharisees (The Established Jewish religion) hated him because he was gathering a following and because he spoke with authority as if he was God. They planned on several occasions to take him and kill him but Jesus escaped them on these occasions. After three years, Judas, one of the disciples betrayed Jesus.

John 18: 2 Now Judas, who betrayed Him, also knew the place, for Jesus often met there with His disciples. 3 So Judas, having taken a detachment of soldiers and officers from the chief priests and Pharisees, came there with lanterns and torches and weapons.

Acts 10: 36 The word which He sent to the children of Israel, preaching peace through Jesus Christ, who is Lord of all, 37 the word, which you know, that was proclaimed throughout all Judea, beginning from Galilee after the baptism which John preached: 38 how God anointed Jesus of Nazareth with the Holy Spirit and with power, who went about doing good and healing all who were oppressed by the devil, for God was with Him.

39 "We are witnesses of all that He did both in the land of the Jews and in Jerusalem, whom they killed by hanging on a tree. 40 But God raised Him on the third day and presented Him publicly, 41 not to all the people, but to witnesses previously chosen by God, to us who ate and drank with Him after He rose from the dead.

He was arrested and abused by Temple guards. He was handed over to the Romans for judgement for penalty of death at proclaiming to be the son of God. Pontias Pilate had him beaten and judged him and sentenced him to death by crucifixion.

John 19: 19 Then Pilate took Jesus and flogged Him. 2 The soldiers twisted a crown of thorns and put it on His head, and they put a purple robe on Him. 3 They said, "Hail, King of the Jews!" And they hit Him with their hands.

4 Again Pilate went out and said to them, "Look, I am bringing Him out to you, that you may know that I find no guilt in Him." 5 Then Jesus came out, wearing the crown of thorns and the purple robe. Pilate said to them,

"Here is the Man!"

6 When the chief priests and officers saw Him, they cried out, "Crucify Him! Crucify Him!"
Pilate said to them, "Take Him yourselves and crucify Him, for I find no guilt in Him."

Jesus' Death – Christians believed the man Jesus Christ literally hung on a cross and died. He had a mortal human body. Other religions teach other things. All Christians believe the truth of this scripture - that Jesus died.

John 19: The Death of Jesus

28 After this, Jesus, knowing that everything was now accomplished, that the Scripture might be fulfilled, said, "I thirst." 29 A bowl full of sour wine was placed there. So they put a sponge full of sour wine on hyssop and held it to His mouth. 30 When Jesus had received the sour wine, He said, "It is finished." And He bowed His head and gave up His spirit.

The Piercing of Jesus' Side

31 Since it was the Day of Preparation, to prevent bodies from remaining on the cross on the Sabbath day (for that Sabbath day was a high day), the Jews asked Pilate that their legs might be broken, and that they might be taken away. 32 Therefore the soldiers came and broke the legs of the first and of the other who was crucified with Him. 33 But when they came to Jesus and saw that He was dead already, they did not break His legs. 34 However, one of the soldiers pierced His side with a spear, and immediately blood and water came out. 35 He who saw it has testified, and his testimony is true. He knows that he is telling the truth, that you may believe. 36 For these things happened so that the Scripture should be fulfilled, "Not one of His bones shall be broken,"[b] 37 and again another Scripture says, "They shall look on Him whom they have pierced."[c]

The Burial of Jesus

38 After this, Joseph of Arimathea, being a disciple of Jesus, but secretly for fear of the Jews, asked Pilate that he might take away the body of Jesus. Pilate gave him permission. So he came and took away His body. 39 Nicodemus, who at first came to Jesus by night, also came, bringing a mixture of myrrh and aloes, weighing about seventy-five pounds.[d] 40 Then they took the body of Jesus and wrapped it in linen cloths with the spices, as is the burial custom of the Jews. 41 Now in the place where He

was crucified there was a garden, and in the garden was a new tomb in which no one had ever been buried. 42 So because of the Jewish Day of Preparation, and since the tomb was nearby, they buried Jesus there.

Not only did Jesus die; he was buried. Joseph of Arimathea gave his tomb for the purpose. It was guarded by Jewish Temple Guards. It was guarded by Roman guards. They guarded it to stop anyone who might steal his body because they had heard that Jesus. There were eye witnesses to prove he was buried and there were official Roman soldiers assigned to guard it. What it means is that aspects of it were recorded by Rome. Rome was known for organization and efficiency and authenticity.

Section 5: He descended to the dead (KJV hell, Sheol Hades Hebrew). On the third day he rose again.

Not only did Jesus die and was buried, his spirit went to the gathering place in the center of the earth that was formerly called Sheol Hades. Jesus said to the thief on the cross who believed in him that he would be with him in Paradise. The place of the dead in the Old Testament. It was a large space with two different sides.

Part of the place of the dead was designated for the unbelieving people: it was known as Sheol Hades or hell.

Part of it was designated for the faithful people of Abraham; it was known as Abraham's Bosom. The gathering place for the dead that was in the centre of the earth is described in Jesus' story about Lazarus and the rich man.

Colossians 2: 13 And you, being dead in your sins and the uncircumcision of your flesh, He has resurrected together with Him, having forgiven you all sins. 14 He blotted out the handwriting of ordinances that was against us and contrary to us, and He took it out of the way, nailing it to the cross. 15 And having disarmed authorities and powers, He made a show of them openly, triumphing over them by the cross.

Luke 16: 19 "There was a rich man who was clothed in purple and fine linen and fared sumptuously every day. 20 There was also a beggar named Lazarus, covered with sores, who had been placed at his gate, 21 desiring to be fed the crumbs falling from the rich man's table. Moreover the dogs came and licked his sores.

22 "It came to pass that the beggar died and was carried by the angels to

Abraham's presence. The rich man also died and was buried. 23 In Hades, being in torment, he lifted up his eyes and saw Abraham from a distance and Lazarus in his presence. 24 So he cried out, 'Father Abraham, have mercy on me, and send Lazarus to dip the tip of his finger in water and cool my tongue. For I am tormented in this flame.'

25 "But Abraham said, 'Son, remember that you in your lifetime received your good things, and Lazarus in like manner evil things. But now he is comforted and you are tormented. 26 And besides all this, between us and you there is a great gulf, so that those who would pass from here to you cannot, nor can those from there pass to us.'

27 "He said, 'Then I pray you, father, to send him to my father's house, 28 for I have five brothers, to testify to them, lest they also come to this place of torment.'

29 "Abraham said to him, 'They have Moses and the Prophets. Let them hear them.'

30 "He said, 'No, father Abraham. But if someone from the dead goes to them, they will repent.'

31 "He said to him, 'If they do not hear Moses and the Prophets, neither will they be persuaded if someone should rise from the dead.' "

The place of Abraham's bosom was a place of peace and rest, while the place of Sheol Hades was an uncomfortable place. It was not the final destiny of unbelievers but it is a place of separation from God which is horrible. Some Christians believe that Jesus went directly to hell, the place of the wicked. Jesus was sentenced to hell because he took upon himself all the sins of the world. But the devil had nothing on Jesus. Jesus had committed no sin. There was no sin in Jesus, so the devil could not keep his soul in Sheol. In fact, Jesus being there, gave him authority over the devil and death and hell.

Revelation 1: 18 I am He who lives, though I was dead. Look! I am alive forevermore. Amen. And I have the keys of Hades and of Death.

Jesus did preach those days his body lay in the tomb. He went into Abraham's Bosom, the place of the righteous believing dead and shared the good news that Messiah had come. The sin of Adam was finally cleansed. They who believed him were rejoicing.

1 Peter 3: 18 For Christ also has once suffered for sins, the just for the unjust, so that He might bring us to God, being put to death in the flesh, but made alive by the Spirit, 19 by whom He also went and preached to the spirits in prison, 20 who in times past were disobedient, when God waited patiently in the days of Noah while the ark was being prepared, in which a few, that is, eight souls, were saved through water.

Abraham's Bosom

That place of the dead is no longer there. Jesus ascended to God and delivered the souls of the righteous dead to be with God in heaven. Only the place of Sheol Hades is still in the center of the earth. The unbeliever who dies goes to that place, awaiting judgement day of the White Throne Judgement which will be after the judgement seat of Christ. They will not be judged as believers.

This scripture explains that at Jesus resurrection, many souls were resurrected. I have only heard rare sermons on this scripture, yet it is an essential truth of the doctrines of Christ.

Matthew 27: 51 At that moment the curtain of the temple was torn in two, from the top to the bottom. And the ground shook, and the rocks split apart. 52 The graves also were opened, and many bodies of the saints who had died were raised, 53 and coming out of the graves after His resurrection, they went into the Holy City and appeared to many.

The righteous dead or believers in Jesus, go to be with Jesus. They await the judgement seat of Christ which will come at the end of this age.

2 Corinthians 5: 8 Instead, I say that we are confident and willing to be absent from the body and to be present with the Lord.

Section 6: He ascended into heaven and is seated at the right hand of the Father.

Jesus was resurrected from the dead. He lived on the earth appearing to people for a period of 40 days. He visibly ascended into heaven in front of over 500 witnesses. They gathered together and saw him rise up in bodily form into the heavens as angels surrounded him.

Acts 1: 7 He said to them, "It is not for you to know the times or the dates, which the Father has fixed by His own authority. 8 But you shall receive power when the Holy Spirit comes upon you. And you shall be My witnesses in Jerusalem, and in all Judea and Samaria, and to the ends of the earth."

9 When He had spoken these things, while they looked, He was taken up. And a cloud received Him from their sight.

10 While they looked intently toward heaven as He ascended, suddenly two men stood by them in white garments. 11 They said, "Men of Galilee, why stand looking toward heaven? This same Jesus, who was taken up from you to heaven, will come in like manner as you saw Him go into heaven."

Jesus is Seated at the Right Hand of God

Jesus is living in his resurrected body in the throne room on a throne seated next to God. Yes, it is true that He is living in believers as the Holy Spirit lives in us but He is not only spirit. He is living in His resurrected body that has a human shape that people on earth witnessed. At the judgement seat of Christ believers will be able to see the nail prints in his hands and feet and the pierce in his side.

Romans 8: 34 Who is he who condemns? It is Christ who died, yes, who is risen, who is also at the right hand of God, who also intercedes for us.

Ephesians 1: 20 which He performed in Christ when He raised Him from the dead and seated Him at His own right hand in the heavenly places, 21 far above all principalities, and power, and might, and dominion, and every name that is named, not only in this age but also in that which is to come.

Colossians 1: 3 If you then were raised with Christ, desire those things which are above, where Christ sits at the right hand of God.

Section 7. He will come again to judge the living and the dead.

Because Jesus died for our sins, without original sin (inherited from Adam) and without any sin of his own, He is worthy to judge. He knows what it is like to live holy as a man. He knows all things concerning human life because he lived as one of us; he died for us; he rose from the dead. He is victor over human life. All who believe in him will be saved.

Matthew 25: 31 "When the Son of Man comes in His glory, and all the holy angels with Him, then He will sit on the throne of His glory. 32 Before Him will be gathered all nations, and He will separate them one from another as a shepherd separates his sheep from the goats. 33 He will set the sheep at

His right hand, but the goats at the left.

2 Corinthians 5: 10 For we must all appear before the judgment seat of Christ, that each one may receive his recompense in the body, according to what he has done, whether it was good or bad.

Revelation 20: 4 I saw thrones, and they sat on them, and the authority to judge was given to them. And I saw the souls of those who had been beheaded for their witness of Jesus and for the word of God. They had not worshipped the beast or his image, and had not received his mark on their foreheads or on their hands. They came to life and reigned with Christ for a thousand years. 5 The rest of the dead did not come to life until the thousand years were ended. This is the first resurrection. 6 Blessed and holy is he who takes part in the first resurrection. Over these the second death has no power, but they shall be priests of God and of Christ and shall reign with Him a thousand years.

Section 8 - I believe in the Holy Spirit,

God promised that He would come and dwell with His people all throughout the Old Testament. Jesus announced that He would send the Holy Spirit to comfort us. As He was ascending in to heaven, he told the believers to go to Jerusalem and wait for the gift of the Holy Spirit.

Jesus spoke of it happening as a prophetic word for the disciples to get.

John 14: 26 But the Counselor, the Holy Spirit, whom the Father will send in My name, will teach you everything and remind you of all that I told you.

Upon His resurrection from the dead, Jesus appeared to the disciples and spoke to them to receive the Holy Spirit.

John 20: 22 When He had said this, He breathed on them and said to them, "Receive the Holy Spirit.

Ascending into heaven, Jesus instructed the disciples to wait for the Holy Spirit.

Acts 1: 8 But you shall receive power when the Holy Spirit comes upon you. And you shall be My witnesses in Jerusalem, and in all Judea and Samaria, and to the ends of the earth."

The disciples who listened to Jesus gathered at Jerusalem not knowing what to expect except that God promised to send the Holy Spirit. 120 of them there, both men and women received the baptism of the Holy Spirit.

Acts 2: 2 Suddenly a sound like a mighty rushing wind came from heaven, and it filled the whole house where they were sitting. 3 There appeared to them tongues as of fire, being distributed and
resting on each of them, 4 and they were all filled with the Holy Spirit and began to speak in other tongues, as the Spirit enabled them to speak.

The disciples who received the baptism of the Holy Spirit were so moved on by God that they left the upper room and went into the streets of Jerusalem speaking in other tongues and worshipping God. They gathered a crowd of people. Some heard them speaking languages from other nations (that they had not learned) and some thought them to be drunk. Peter preached the truth that God had sent the Holy Spirit as He promised in Joel 2: 28. He preached Jesus Christ as Lord to them. Consequently, thousands of pilgrims who had come to Jerusalem to worship God for the feast of Pentecost received Jesus Christ as Saviour and Lord and were baptised with the Holy Spirit. It is clearly promised to all people who would believe (including us).

Acts 2: 38 Peter said to them, "Repent and be baptized, every one of you, in the name of Jesus Christ for the forgiveness of sins, and you shall receive the gift of the Holy Spirit. 39 For the promise is to you, and to your children, and to all who are far away, as many as the Lord our God will call."

40 With many other words he testified and exhorted them, saying, "Be saved from this perverse generation." 41 Then those who gladly received his word were baptized, and that day about three thousand souls were added to them.

Section 9: the holy Catholic (universal - my emphasis) Church, the communion of saints,

The words Roman Catholic Church do not appear in scripture. The meaning of the word Catholic is universal or worldwide. It means that all Christians who believe these essential truths although they may be different in denomination etc. are part of the One True Church.

If you believe Jesus Christ is Lord, you are a member of the body of Christ.

1 Corinthians 12: 27 Now you are the body of Christ and members individually.

The Apostle Paul referred to the Church to talk about all the Christians.

1Timothy 3: 15 but if I am delayed, you might know how you ought to conduct yourself in the house of God, which is the church of the living God, the pillar and foundation of the truth.

Jesus gave his life for the Church or people who would believe in him.

Ephesians 5: 25 Husbands, love your wives, just as Christ also loved the church and gave Himself for it, 26 that He might sanctify and cleanse it with the washing of water by the word, 27 and that He might present to Himself a glorious church, not having spot, or wrinkle, or any such thing, but that it should be holy and without blemish.

All the saints will be with God in a new Jerusalem in a new heavens and earth. The Church is compared to a bride – being pure and devout.

Revelation 21: 1 Then I saw "a new heaven and a new earth."[a] For the first heaven and the first earth had passed away, and there was no more sea. 2 I, John, saw the Holy City, the New Jerusalem, coming down out of heaven from God, prepared as a bride adorned for her husband.

Section 10 - the forgiveness of sins,

Believing on the LORD Jesus Christ who died in our place so that we might be made right with God is the core belief of Christianity. Jesus died for our sins. We believe that Jesus died taking upon Himself all sin and curse that was the result of Adam's sin. If we repent or turn to God, God forgives us and cleanses us and makes it as though we have never sinned. It is known as the doctrine of Justification.

Romans 10: 13 For, "Everyone who calls on the name of the Lord shall be saved."[f]

1 John 1: 7 But if we walk in the light as He is in the light, we have fellowship one with another, and the blood of Jesus Christ His Son cleanses us from all sin.

Section 11 - 11. the resurrection of the body,

Acts 24: 15 I have hope in God that there will be a resurrection of the dead, both of the just and the unjust, which they also expect. 16 In this do I always strive to have a clear conscience toward God and toward men.

Romans 6: the resurrection of the dead, and eternal judgment.

The first resurrection or resurrection of the just (believers in Jesus).

Revelation 20: 4 I saw thrones, and they sat on them, and the authority to judge was given to them. And I saw the souls of those who had been beheaded for their witness of Jesus and for the word of God. They had not worshipped the beast or his image, and had not received his mark on their foreheads or on their hands. They came to life and reigned with Christ for a thousand years. 5 The rest of the dead did not come to life until the thousand years were ended. This is the first resurrection. 6 Blessed and holy is he who takes part in the first resurrection. Over these the second death has no power, but they shall be priests of God and of Christ and shall reign with Him a thousand years.

The second resurrection or the White Throne Judgement – the resurrection of non-believers.

Revelation 20: 11 Then I saw a great white throne and Him who was seated on it. From His face the earth and the heavens fled away, and no place was found for them. 12 And I saw the dead, small and great, standing before God. Books were opened. Then another book was opened, which is the Book of Life. The dead were judged according to their works as recorded in the books. 13 The sea gave up the dead who were in it, and Death and Hades delivered up the dead who were in them. And they were judged, each one by his works. 14 Then Death and Hades were cast into the lake of fire. This is the second death. 15 Anyone whose name was not found written in the Book of Life was cast into the lake of fire.

Section 12 and the life everlasting.

Humans were created to live eternally with God as friends of God. Because of Adam`s sin against God, we were separated from God. Only through Jesus life, death, burial and resurrection was man made clearly pure to be in God`s Holy presence.

Jesus promised eternal life to the woman at the well.

The Bible clearly teaches that all humans will live forever. The main purpose for sharing Jesus with others is that we know there is eternal life. Believers will live in eternal joy while unbelievers will suffer torment.

John 4: 13 Jesus said to her, "Everyone who drinks of this water will thirst again, 14 but whoever drinks of the water that I shall give him will never thirst. Indeed, the water that I shall give him will become in him a well of water springing up into eternal life."

Revelation 22: The throne of God and of the Lamb shall be in it, and His servants shall serve Him. 4 They shall see His face, and His name shall be on their foreheads. 5 Night shall be no more. They need no lamp nor the light of the sun, for the Lord God will give them light. And they shall reign forever and ever.

Believing these key aspects of the Christian faith are essential for a Church to be considered a Christian church. Although it was established almost 2, 000 years ago, all main line Christian Churches agree on these truths.

3 THE DOCTRINE OF CHRIST
REPENTACE AND FAITH TOWARDS GOD

Chapter 3

Hebrews 6: 1 Therefore, leaving the elementary principles of the doctrine of Christ, let us go on to maturity, not laying again a foundation of repentance from dead works and of faith toward God, 2 of instruction about washings, the laying on of hands, the resurrection of the dead, and eternal judgment. 3 This we will do if God permits.

The scripture above is one that summarizes the main aspects of the Christian faith. It is essential that a Christian build a firm foundation of truths in his or her spiritual life. I am fascinated by construction. I like to watch construction workers digging with giant earth moving machines and pouring a cement foundation. Next. they begin construction with metal beams and braces. I am sure part of my attraction to is that my dad was in construction. He would often show us buildings that he helped to build including malls, shopping centers, schools etc. What I learned is that the deeper the digging, meant the taller the building. The truth also applies to us spiritually. The more sure and strong the foundation, the more we can build on these truths.

1 Corinthians 3: 10 According to the grace of God which has been given to me, as a wise master builder, I have laid the foundation, but another builds on it. Now let each one take heed how he builds on it. 11 For no one can lay another foundation than that which was laid, which is Jesus Christ. 12 Now if anyone builds on this foundation with gold, silver, precious stones, wood, hay, or stubble, 13 each one's work will be revealed.

The list of truths in Hebrews 6 includes the main stones of our Christian faith or the foundations of what a Christian believes. You will notice a consistency with these foundation stones and the Apostle's Creed.

Repentance

Repentance is not possible unless the Holy Spirit draws you to God. Usually it is because you have prayed asking God to show you that He is real or because someone is praying for you. What happens is that your heart becomes softer towards the things of God. Where you may have rejected the idea of knowing the God of the Bible in your past, suddenly, you desire to know the truths of God believing that if there is a true God, you would be helped.

Before repentance comes a drawing unto God. You may desire to read God's Word. You may watch a television preacher. You may talk to some Christians you know. You may seek a church. You will desire God, the way someone seeking a treasure would draw close as possible to all the clues and diligently seek knowing the treasure is worth it. You must be truly seeking God for Him to reveal Himself to you.

It is while your heart is softened or drawn to know the truth that God will use any manner of communication to touch your heart with the core truth of salvation. You may hear one of these scriptures and respond with faith towards God. God promises that if we should earnestly seek Him, He will be found of us. Some people believe finding God is really tough and it is a lifelong quest. That isn't true, but you have got to be searching in the right sources.

Testimony (brief version)

I always believed there was God but I didn't know how to find God. I prayed believing God heard me. In my teenage years and early twenties, I pursued God with passion. I read books about most major religions. I studied Eastern religion and especially was interested in life after death. Although I studied these things, I did not feel a sense of peace. I did not believe I had the answer. I would often talk with other teen agers about life after death and God. They were as interested in the topic as I was. None of us had the answers. I did not turn to God of the Bible because I believed the lie that Christianity was just a bunch of laws and had no substance.

I studied the occult and often read people's fortunes and horoscopes from them. I invested hundreds of dollars in these books. I had some supernatural gifts and I enjoyed doing it. Finally, when I most needed God, I turned to Jehovah God. I began reading scriptures and praying. I had a supernatural encounter with God that changed my life forever.

There were some Christians praying for me. I didn't know it of course. They would always ask me to go to church with them but I didn't want to. I was not raised a Christian. After the encounter with God, a supernatural encounter with those Christian family of my friend came into my life at a point of a destiny decision. I went with them. I accepted Jesus Christ as

Saviour and LORD by praying with them. I felt a weight roll off me as though I were suddenly free. I knew that Jesus was really God and there was nothing separating me from God because I confessed that I was a sinner and in need of forgiveness. They explained to me how Jesus died for my sins so I could be free from sin.

Suddenly, there was a radical change in my life. The very next day, I knew I had to burn the occult books. God's Spirit was on the inside of me and I knew I had to get rid of things that would not draw me closer to God. I also got rid of records and music, magazines etc. The Holy Spirit was living in me. I was not alone. I knew God was in me and it comforted me beyond what any words could express. God would prompt me and speak to me and I felt a sense of peace that I had never known before. True repentance had come to me. I received the truth of Jesus Christ and was transformed by it.

Jeremiah 29: 13 You shall seek Me and find Me, when you shall search for Me with all your heart.

James 4: 8 Draw near to God, and He will draw near to you. Cleanse your hands, you sinners, and purify your hearts, you double-minded.

John 3: 16 "For God so loved the world that He gave His only begotten Son, that whoever believes in Him should not perish, but have eternal life. 17 For God did not send His Son into the world to condemn the world, but that the world through Him might be saved.

Romans 10: This is the word of faith that we preach: 9 that if you confess with your mouth Jesus is Lord, and believe in your heart that God has raised Him from the dead, you will be saved, 10 for with the heart one believes unto righteousness, and with the mouth confession is made unto salvation.

Romans 10: 13 For, "Everyone who calls on the name of the Lord shall be saved."[f]

I can truly speak with any person who believes there is no hope for him or her in finding God. I know that if God could make himself known to me, that I could be saved, any person on earth could be saved. I know that God saved me from the uttermost – how I interpret it is that I was searching in all the wrong places for God, yet God still had mercy on me and revealed himself to me.

Hebrews 7: 25 25 Therefore He is able to save to the uttermost those who come to God through Him, because He at all times lives to make intercession for them.

Right after my salvation, my life became different. Things that were once part of my life, I either cut off or stopped doing. People who once were in my life either were completely repulsive to me or I was now completely repulsive to them. I shared my testimony with almost everyone I knew. Before the end of the first week of my salvation I had brought a friend to Christ by my testimony. She knew that I was searching for God. She knew of all of the different religions I had studied searching. She also saw the change in me. I was a different person. I was free.

I only include this testimony to give you hope. If you are reading this book and do not yet know Jesus as Saviour and Lord, you can know Him. Literally pray out loud " God, if it is really true, reveal yourself to me. Lord Jesus Christ, I want to know you. Reveal yourself to me. Bring people into my life that can help me. Direct me to people who can help me." If you pray that simple prayer, expect God to lead you to the right people. You may feel a certain prompting in your spirit to attend a church. Don't just go anywhere. Go to a place where they literally believe the Bible and believe in the gifts of the Holy Spirit. The awesome thing about the Internet is that it can be used for preaching. If you don't know where to find out more about God, go to Trinity Broadcasting Network on the Internet. There is 24/7 Christian programming. There is preaching and teaching by strong Christian leaders who can speak life into your spirit and inspire you.
That is a place to start.

If you once were a Christian but now are not living a Christian life. There is hope for you. The same Jesus that saved me will reveal Himself to you. It requires repentance. I have known people who have been close to God, but because of something that happened, they no longer believe they are worthy to be a Christian. It doesn't matter what you have done; God can forgive you. There is no person worthy of salvation. That is the awesome things about Jesus Christ. He came to save sinners not righteous people.

Sin

There are two types of sin that a person has: original sin (the inherited sin from Adam and Eve's disobedience to God) and willful sin or doing things that are wrong even though you know they are wrong. God's plan for Adam and Eve did not include death. They were created and placed in the Garden of Eden to procreate and to enjoy the garden. There were animals, fruit trees and all types of vegetation. There were no weeds, no thorns, no thistles. There was no evil, no sin; all things were in harmony with God. Each day God's presence would come and talk with them in the cool of the day or evening. They enjoyed a life of blessing that was prepared by them and give to them by God. They were free to eat of any of the trees except one. God commanded Adam not to eat from the tree of Good and evil. God made it clear. It was the one thing God said they couldn't have.

Genesis 3: 4 Then the serpent said to the woman, "You surely will not die! 5 For God knows that on the day you eat of it your eyes will be opened and you will be like God, knowing good and evil."

6 When the woman saw that the tree was good for food, that it was pleasing to the eyes and a tree desirable to make one wise, she took of its fruit and ate; and she gave to her husband with her, and he ate. 7 Then the eyes of both were opened, and they knew that they were naked. So they sewed fig leaves together and made coverings for themselves.

There was a serpent in the garden and it spoke to Eve because Satan possessed it. He used God's words and twisted them and accused God of trying to keep knowledge and power from them. He said it would make them like gods. This is a direct accusation that God wanted them to be subordinate. Those words stuck in the woman. She started looking at the fruit on the tree and desiring it. Both Eve and Adam were seduced into sin of taking that forbidden fruit. They both had it. Immediately they both knew they were naked. I believe because of their sin, their covering was taken off them. The covering would have been like the glory of God on them. They were naked but didn't know it or care about it because they were innocent and clothed with God's presence.

Because of this sin – sin entered the human race. Adam and Eve were the first – but all people who were born after them were born with this sin – original sin. Even the most innocent child has original sin. That is why we must personally encounter Jesus Christ and come to know him as Saviour. Jesus saves us from the curse of Adam.

Because of their disobedience, God judged Adam and Eve. They did not die immediately but their spirits died in relationship with God. They lived many years afterwards but there was sin in all of their children and in all people because of their rebellion against God.

These were the judgements on the people: They were banished from the Garden of Eden and had to live outside of the beautiful place God had made them.

Genesis 3: 16 To the woman He said,
"I will greatly multiply your pain in childbirth,
    and in pain you will bring forth children;
your desire will be for your husband,
    and he will rule over you."

17 And to Adam He said, "Because you have listened to the voice of your wife and have eaten from the tree about which I commanded you, saying, 'You shall not eat of it,'
Cursed is the ground on account of you;
    in hard labor you will eat of it
    all the days of your life.
18 Thorns and thistles it will bring forth for you,
    and you will eat the plants of the field.
19 By the sweat of your face
    you will eat bread
until you return to the ground,
    because out of it you were taken;
for you are dust,
    and to dust you will return."

The curse of Adam and Eve's sins covered all areas of their lives: from bearing children, family relationships, labour or work as well as a curse on the earth including the animals. The only hope was promised as part of the serpent's curse –

Genesis 3:
15 I will put enmity
    between you and the woman,
    and between your offspring and her offspring;
he will bruise your head,
    and you will bruise his heel."

One day, a seed of the man and the woman would rise up and crush the head of the serpent. This was not only speaking about that animal but about the coming of a Saviour who would crush Satan's head and give freedom to people once more. Throughout the thousands of years until the birth of Jesus, the hope of God's people was the news of the Messiah or Saviour who would come and restore relationship with man once more.

Throughout these thousands of years, God made covenants or promises to different people of faith that were promises to people if they obeyed God's commandments.

Please know that God prepared the answer to man's sin, before the foundations of the earth, because he knew that man would sin (Revelation 13: 8) . God gave Jesus Christ as the sacrifice to pay the penalty of Adam. No person except Jesus could pay the price. First the person had to be without original sin. All people born of Adam had original sin. Jesus was born of the virgin Mary; he had no inherited sin from Adam. He lived a holy life. He was tempted but did not sin   (Hebrews 4: 15). He willingly gave his life to take upon himself all the sins of all people, past and present and future. It meant that he was accused and found guilty, but he did no crime. He was sentenced to death. He died on the cross, but he rose from the dead with victory over sin and hell and death.

The other type of sin is willful sin. It is direct sin against God by disobeying the commandments.

Exodus 20:
1Now God spoke all these words, saying:
2 I am the Lord your God, who brought you out of the land of Egypt, out of the house of bondage.
3 You shall have no other gods before Me.
4 You shall not make for yourself any graven idol, or any likeness of anything that is in heaven above, or that is in the earth beneath, or that is in the water below the earth. 5 You shall not bow down to them or serve them; for I, the Lord your God, am a jealous God, visiting the iniquity of the fathers on the children to the third and fourth generation of them who hate Me, 6 and showing lovingkindness to thousands of them who love Me and keep My commandments.

7 You shall not take the name of the Lord your God in vain, for the Lord will not hold guiltless anyone who takes His name in vain.
8 Remember the Sabbath day and keep it holy. 9 Six days you shall labor and do all your work, 10 but the seventh day is a Sabbath to the Lord your God. On it you shall not do any work, you, or your son, or your daughter, or your male servant, or your female servant, or your livestock, or your sojourner who is within your gates. 11 For in six days the Lord made heaven and earth, the sea, and all that is in them, and rested on the seventh day. Therefore, the Lord blessed the Sabbath day and made it holy.
12 Honor your father and your mother, that your days may be long in the land which the Lord your God is giving you.

13 You shall not murder.

14 You shall not commit adultery.

15 You shall not steal.

16 You shall not bear false witness against your neighbor.

17 You shall not covet your neighbor's house; you shall not covet your neighbor's wife, or his manservant, or his maidservant, or his ox, or his donkey, or anything that is your neighbor's.

The commandments that gave God to Moses at first were the ones above. They covered all aspects of human life. Later more commandments were given (613) to give order for society and daily life of all aspects of human life. The microcosm of them is in the original commandments. Sin is the disobedience of any of these commandments. Jesus was the only person whoever kept all the commandments all his life without sin. Jesus paid the penalty for all sin so that we might be set free. Faith in Jesus Christ means freedom to worship, freedom to commune with God, direct access to God and freedom from all the curse of Adam. We can know life of blessing, prosperity, health and joy in communion with God.

Here is the Apostle Paul's testimony in brief.

If you know anything about the Apostle Paul, you know that he was well educated. He knew the scriptures. He was revered by the religious people in his society. He was passionate, but he was misguided. He wanted to persecute Christians because he believed he was right. Only when the LORD Jesus Christ appeared to him and spoke to him directly did he change. The change was immediate. After he had met Jesus Christ, his life was transformed.

1 Timothy 1: 12 I thank Christ Jesus our Lord, who has enabled me, because He counted me faithful and appointed me to the ministry. 13 I was previously a blasphemer, and a persecutor, and an insolent man. But I was shown mercy, because I did it ignorantly in unbelief. 14 The grace of our Lord overflowed with the faith and love which is in Christ Jesus.

15 This is a faithful saying and worthy of all acceptance, that Christ Jesus came into the world to save sinners, of whom I am the worst. 16 But I received mercy for this reason, that in me, first, Jesus Christ might show all patience, as an example to those who were to believe in Him for eternal life.

You once knew God but

If you once knew God, the same Jesus that forgave you in the past is ready to receive you in the present. It is no coincidence you are reading my book. Please take a moment. Thank God for softening your heart. Ask Him to forgive you. Don't believe the lie that any sin can't be forgiven. Jesus blood was shed for all types of sin for all people who ever lived in the past, in the present or in the future. Jesus died once. He was Holy. He never sinned. His blood was shed by his own free will. He died to take your place. He died to take my place so that I could be free to communicate with God.

Hebrews 10: 14 For by one offering He has forever perfected those who are sanctified.

15 The Holy Spirit also witnesses to us about this. For after saying,
 16 "This is the covenant that I will make with them
    after those days, says the Lord:
I will put My laws into their hearts,
    and in their minds I will write them,"[d]
 17 then He adds,
"Their sins and lawless deeds
    will I remember no more."[e]
 18 Now where there is forgiveness of these, there is no longer an offering for sin.

You can be set free

Don't believe any lie that you can't break a sinful habit or addiction. There is always hope as long as you live. You need to get with the right people. If the place you are in there are no people teaching or preaching freedom to live a holy life with signs and wonders following, you are not in the right place. First, repent and ask God to forgive you and help you find the right people. Until it occurs, start watching that Christian Network I told you about (TBN). You will hear a different kind of preaching on it. There will be people preaching salvation, deliverance and healing with faith.

Deliverance means freedom from sin or addiction or bondage. You can be healed completely, in your body or soul. God can completely heal you and give you a new beginning of life no matter what may have happened to you. You can be completely healed so that although you may know what happened to you, there is no sting to it any more. I would describe it as being stung by a bee that not only hurts once, but the stinger in you makes all the flesh red and sore around it. God can pull out the stinger so there is no pain associated with it any more.

Laying the foundation stone of repentance and faith towards God must be done by faith in Christ. You cannot do it in your own strength. It is not a mental ascent. All in the kingdom of God is by faith in Jesus Christ. You must realize that you cannot do it on your own and that only by God's grace in Jesus Christ is it possible. Once you are humble in your heart, you can be ready to receive from God.

Hebrews 11: 6 And without faith it is impossible to please God, for he who comes to God must believe that He exists and that He is a rewarder of those who diligently seek Him.

Not Dead Works

Some people believe that they can perhaps do things to gain points with God. They believe that if they will do certain things, pray certain prayers, or go to so many services a week, or do good deeds, they can earn their way to heaven or to higher levels of faith. All of those things I've mentioned are dead works. What it means is that there is nothing you can do to make yourself more holy. There is nothing you can do to earn points with God. God clearly lets us know if it is not of faith – it is sin.

Romans 14: 23 But he who doubts is condemned if he eats, because it is not from faith, for whatever is not from faith is sin.

Ephesians 2: 8 For by grace you have been saved through faith, and this is not of yourselves. It is the gift of God, 9 not of works, so that no one should boast.

There is nothing you can do outwardly that can make God love you more or love you less. Jesus gave us the best he could give – he gave us his life so we could be free. Anything that you try to do to make yourself more holy is a sin. There is nothing you can do that will make yourself more right with God. It can't come by giving, or doing or any outward way.

The Blood of Jesus

Only Jesus blood can make you holy. You must receive by faith. If necessary say it out loud. " God I receive by faith your blood cleansing me from all sin. I am made holy by your blood. I receive it." God says that our own righteousness is as filthy menstrual cloths. The best we could give would never be enough to make us holy. Only through the blood of Jesus that you receive by faith can you be made pure. It comes by faith.

Isaiah 64: 6 But we all are as an unclean thing,

and all our righteousness is as filthy rags;
and we all fade as a leaf,
    and our iniquities, like the wind, have taken us away.

There were days in my life I had to speak scripture to my own self so I could hear it. Faith comes by hearing the word of God. If you can't stop thinking that you are a sinner after you have confessed your sins, start speaking scripture to yourself out loud. You are not forgiven because you feel forgiven. You are forgiven because God says so in His word. What is in the Bible is God's promises to us. It shows his will for all people. Start saying to yourself the following scripture.

2 Corinthians 5: 21 God made Him who knew no sin to be sin for us, that we might become the righteousness of God in Him.

After your repented and received Jesus Christ, stop saying you are a sinner. You were a sinner, but you have been saved by grace. You are the righteousness of God in Jesus Christ. If you sin, repent quickly and start confessing again that you are the righteousness of God in Christ. You have got to get the word of God in the deep inward parts of your being. The word of God must become a part of you. Simply memorizing it isn't enough. Say it out loud so you can hear it with your ears. You do it so you can hear your own voice saying it. The word of God gets into your innermost spirit man and what happens is that you are truly transformed by it.

Don't let anyone deceive you with false teachings.

As soon as you give yourself to God, you should start praying for discerning of spirits so you may know God's voice different from any other. It is essential to get into an excellent local church that preaches and teaches the truths I am speaking about. There are millions of Christians in North America. There are thousands of excellent churches. Find one that preaches and teaches the truths of Christ. It is important so that you get the foundations but also that you get connected with people who share the same faith – the Bible uses the term "like precious faith". You can learn and give and serve and become as part of a spiritual family. It is essential that you get excellent teaching and preaching. Don't just listen to any preacher on television. You notice I gave the name of a network TBN. I do it for this reason; all the preaching and teaching on that network is lined up with God's word. I cannot speak the same of all preachers on all television.

Colossians 2: 8 Beware lest anyone captivate you through philosophy and vain deceit, in the tradition of men and the elementary principles of the world, and not after Christ.

There is no philosophy or path to heaven that man can make. There is no path that humans can create to make us closer to God. Ideas that man has created cannot give us true spiritual revelation or enlightenment. There is only one way to God: it is through Jesus Christ. He is the way, the truth and the life (John 14: 6). You can only come to God through Christ. Don't depart from the faith. Don't believe you must add something to the simple acceptance of Jesus blood.

Don't believe anything you can do can make yourself more spiritual or more Holy. There is no tradition of men that can save you or redeem you. Keep thanking God for your salvation: it comes through faith in Jesus Christ.! Let it constantly release joy in you. The joy I'm speaking of is you know that God showed you mercy and has forgiven you and changed you because of His grace. You know it is all a gift of God, not of your own self. Maintain an attitude of thanking God for simple things as well as big things. Titus 3: 5 not by works of righteousness which we have done, but according to His mercy He saved us, through the washing of rebirth and the renewal of the Holy Spirit, 6 whom He poured out on us abundantly through Jesus Christ our Savior, 7 so that, being justified by His grace, we might become heirs according to the hope of eternal life.

The above scripture helps us to understand that salvation and spiritual growth and all to do with our spiritual life comes as a free gift of God.

Water Baptism in itself does not make you righteous. I will talk about it in a different teaching. Water baptism makes you obedient to what God has commanded. It is an expression of our faith. Getting dunked under the water is just that, unless there is faith that you are surrendering all your life to God. None of the sacraments can make you holy or righteous. They are things we do to show our faith in God. We do them in obedience to the commandments of God and the things Jesus taught us. Faith in Jesus Christ is essential for the sacrament to have any spiritual significance to us. I do a detailed teaching on the sacraments in a different book.

Paying your way

There was a dark period in the church history where there was much corruption in the organized church and people were told that by giving so much money, they could pay their way out of hell. They were sold pieces of paper that insured their salvation. Other false teachers taught that by buying relics of saints (real or fake) such a saint's bone or piece of clothing etc. could make them holier and closer to God. Unfortunately, there are still false teachers who use this very same technique of making people believe they can give their way out of eternal judgement. Most people who don't know God, know they are not right with God. Most of those people condemn themselves and many of them believe they are unworthy to be a Christian.

These people need to get the truth of salvation through Jesus Christ alone. They need to see how awesome the gift of grace is. Our God is so good that even when there was no way for us to get to Him, He came to us as a human baby, lived a holy life, suffered and died to take our place. He rose from the dead and to all who will believe He will freely give the gift of eternal life. It doesn't make logical sense. It isn't levels of salvation. It is instant. As soon as you repent and receive Jesus Christ as your Saviour and Lord, you are saved. It is too easy for most people to believe. It is free – it is the gift of God – grace.

No serving to get to heaven

I was not raised in a Christian home. I had relatives who would sometimes go to church on Christmas or Easter because they thought it would make them right with God although they didn't live A Christian life or profess God any other occasion. If they truly were seeking God on those occasions, only God Himself knows. God honours people's faith.

There are people who are in religions that mention Jesus Christ but do not honour Him as God or LORD. In some of those cults the people literally believe that if they do not share their faith with so many people a day, they will not make it to heaven. They believe their good works earn them a place in heaven.

I am strongly stating and emphasizing that there is no possible way you can make yourself more holy or more pleasing to God through your works. If the thought at all arises in your heart that what you are doing earns you points with God, you have got to repent of it.

Repentance

Repentance means you confess it is wrong. You ask God to forgive you. You turn from that way of sin and give yourself to serving God wholly. You no longer do that sinful thing. It is the transformation of a life. Repentance is something that can be witnessed by others because your life changes. Your habits change; the things you do changes. It can be something like murder or lying or stealing but dead works is also a sin. Whatever is not of faith is sin.

Pleading the Blood

Pleading the blood is important. Let me explain it to you. It is an older term used by people of faith. It means literally as though you were a convicted criminal and were in a court room and you were asked what you plead, you would plead the blood. Plead means – if you are guilty say so; if you are innocent say so. There is an alternative. You plead the blood of Jesus. You know that you have no righteousness in your own self. If you were to stand before God in your own strength, you would clearly be a sinner, but you do not stand in your own strength. You believe so strongly in the blood of Jesus shed for you that it is your plea. It is your hope. It is your faith – Jesus righteousness given to you by his mercy towards you, giving you access to God and imparting or giving you the righteousness of God. Jesus righteousness is your righteousness because you freely accept the offering Jesus gave.

Justification

The term justification not used much anymore in the Pentecostal churches that I know of but it is really important because what it means is that you have repented and Jesus blood has cleansed you. The blood of Jesus erases you sin as though it never existed. This is important because all the covenants that God made with man were dependent on some type of animal sacrifice that could not atone or erase your sin. It was God's way of letting us know that one day Jesus the Messiah would come and die for us so that we could have communion with God – friendship with God. The animal sacrifice was like a placeholder or a book mark – indicating one day Messiah will come and forgive all sins. Jesus the Messiah's blood was offered once and for all people. It is the only possible way to erase sin.

I don't know if you play sports, but if you do and you are with a friend and you are playing for fun and you mess up. For instance, I have played golf and the first tee off, the ball was less than 9 feet away. I would say "do over" and what it would mean is that I would redo my shot. Many people are so competitive this type of thing I am speaking of is offensive to them. It is a fresh start, a new opportunity. There are many people in life who believe that they have ruined their lives and there is no answer for them but death. Some of these people are in prison for life for committing terrible crimes. Some of these people are living lonely lives because of a divorce or a bad decision etc.

The Good News

If you believe on the Lord Jesus Christ, you will be saved. (Romans 10:9)

The good news or the gospel is to be shared with these people. There is hope for them through Jesus Christ. There is always a do over with Jesus. There is always a fresh start. Even if you screw up, God will forgive you if you truly repent. You do not have to believe the lie that you can never be successful or happy. Most of the ministries I am partners with contribute to sending or giving to prisons. I myself have ministered in such a situation. You share the good news of forgiveness with these people and Jesus hope for them and they can be set free. I could see the twinkle of hope come into the people I spoke with. They received hope in a situation where they believed there was no answer.

I like what the Evangelist Jesse Duplantis says frequently "Failure is not an option." What it means is there is always a way with God. All things are possible with our God, because He is really God. I am saying the prison building itself is not the worst part of their lives. If you can believe on the LORD Jesus Christ and his blood shed for you, and start reading the Bible and praying and living a life serving God, you can be free no matter where you are. There are some people who are in prison but who have accepted Christ and they are truly free. They share Jesus Christ with the people around them. They evangelize within the prison. I have read testimonies of people's lives transformed because of Jesus Christ setting them free to be joyful and to know true peace.

Jesus explained this life transformation to one of the Pharisees who went to him believing he was a teacher from God. Jesus told him he needed rebirth in his spirit. Literally it means, repent. Accept Jesus as the only way to eternal life. Receive the blessings from it and start your life fresh with God.

John 3: 3 Jesus answered him, "Truly, truly I say to you, unless a man is born again,[a] he cannot see the kingdom of God."

4 Nicodemus said to Him, "How can a man be born when he is old? Can he enter a second time into his mother's womb and be born?"

5 Jesus answered, "Truly, truly I say to you, unless a man is born of water

and the Spirit, he cannot enter the kingdom of God. 6 That which is born of the flesh is flesh, and that which is born of the Spirit is spirit. 7 Do not marvel that I said to you, 'You must be born again.' 8 The wind blows where it wishes, and you hear its sound, but you do not know where it comes from or where it goes. So it is with everyone who is born of the Spirit."

Living your Faith

Your faith will be evident in your life. It will be evident in your beliefs, habits, conversation, commitments, giving, and things you do. You do not help the needy or the poor because you do it to be holy. Because you are a Christian, you start loving other people so strongly, you want to give to help them. You want to serve them. You want to make a difference. Jesus commands us to obey the commandments and he summarizes all of the commandments in his words.

Mark 12: 29 Jesus answered him, "The first of all the commandments is, 'Hear, O Israel, the Lord our God is one Lord. 30 You shall love the Lord your God with all your heart, and with all your soul, and with all your mind, and with all your strength.'[d] This is the first commandment. 31 The second is this: 'You shall love your neighbor as yourself.'[e] There is no other commandment greater than these."

Once more, I want to explain, you don't start serving or giving to others because you believe it makes you spiritual. What happens when you give yourself wholly to God is that the agape (Greek for God kind of love or unconditional) love of God, the overwhelming love of God fills you and brings you such joy that you start loving people more than you have ever in the past. The Holy Spirit inside of you is God in you. You will feel godly compassion for people. You will feel concern as though all people are your concern – because God who lives in you is expressing the love of God towards people.

If you have truly given yourself wholly to God, you will feel overwhelming mercy towards people. You will realize the purpose you are on earth is to serve, to give, to express love, to do something that can help others. You will feel a connectedness with all people. The agape love of God is God's love loving people through your spirit. It will be evident in how you live your life.

Good works

The fruit of a tree often is the indicator on what type of tree it is. What we talk about most reveals your heart. What you do with your life, reveals your priorities.

Luke 6: 43 "A good tree does not bear corrupt fruit, nor does a corrupt tree bear good fruit. 44 Each tree is known by its own fruit. Men do not gather figs from thorns, nor do they gather grapes from a wild bush. 45 A good man out of the good treasure of his heart bears what is good, and an evil man out of the evil treasure of his heart bears what is evil. For of the abundance of the heart his mouth speaks.

Certain things are evident in mature Christians' lives. They are evidence of the fruit of their love for God and relationship with Him. They develop godly character. Examples of godly character are below. They are proof of God living in us. They are character qualities like God. We should desire them and pray that God would transform us so these qualities are in us. They will cause people to know there is something different about us. They will cause people to want to know Jesus.

Galatians 5: 22 But the fruit of the Spirit is love, joy, peace, patience, gentleness, goodness, faith, 23 meekness, and self-control; against such there is no law.

The motive for what you do matters. You are not doing it to gain a place with God. You've got communion with God and because of it- you give because Jesus Christ lives in you and through you. Because of God literally transforming us or changing us from glory to glory, we will be recognized by our giving, serving, mercy, kindness, gentleness etc. towards people. It will include caring for those who are poor or needy. The giving of mercy and alms and caring for those who could never repay you is God's expression of love through is people on the earth. People should recognize us as Christians because of the evidence in our words, our character, and our giving and serving.

Ephesians 2: 10 For we are His workmanship, created in Christ Jesus for good works, which God prepared beforehand, so that we should walk in them.

James 2: 14 What does it profit, my brothers, if a man says he has faith but has no works? Can faith save him? 15 If a brother or sister is naked and lacking daily food, 16 and one of you says to them, "Depart in peace, be warmed and filled," and yet you give them nothing that the body needs, what does it profit? 17 So faith by itself, if it has no works, is dead.

Are you right with God?

If you are reading this book, I don't believe it is a coincidence. Are you right with God? Without any hesitation, you can say that you are living in communion with God. If you cannot say it with truth, you can repent right now – and know you are right with God. If you are not sure, you can get right with God and of a certainty know that you are right with Him. Sin separates us from God. If you are in right relationship with God, you will be in communion with God. You will be friends with God. You will be talking to Him and He will be talking to you. You will have peace beyond all human explanation. You will have joy that overflows bubbling up from your spirit within you because God's Holy Spirit will be living in you and quickening you. It is easy. If you are not sure that you are right with God pray. Sin is anything that you know is wrong that you have done against God or people. Confess your sin and believe that Jesus blood cleanses you. Start living for God.

1 John 1: 7 But if we walk in the light as He is in the light, we have fellowship one with another, and the blood of Jesus Christ His Son cleanses us from all sin.

4 DOCTRINE OF BAPTISMS

Chapter 4

Hebrews 6: 1Therefore, leaving the elementary principles of the doctrine of Christ, let us go on to maturity, not laying again a foundation of repentance from dead works and of faith toward God, 2 of instruction about washings, the laying on of hands, the resurrection of the dead, and eternal judgment. 3 This we will do if God permits.

Water Baptism
Water Baptism – taken from my book on the Sacraments

Entering the New Covenant with God

Hebrews 6 includes the foundational doctrines of the Christine Church. Water Baptism is one of these foundational stones and is also a sacrament. If you haven't been water baptized but you are a Christian, this teaching is prompting for you to obey the LORD and get water Baptized. The purpose of this teaching is to explain why you should be water baptized if you are a Christian. This is in obedience to Jesus and the New Covenant that He brought us through his death, burial and resurrection.

The Old Testament

The Old Covenant is associated with Moses and the commandments that God gave to Moses for the people. The New covenant came through Jesus Christ the Messiah who fulfilled all the laws of Moses by living a Holy life, completely without sin, and who died for us taking our sins and inequities upon himself. He died; He was buried; on the third day, He arose from the dead triumphant over death, hell and the grave. Jesus is the promised Messiah that is mentioned throughout all of the Old Testament. He fulfilled all the prophecies of the Messiah.

Under the Old Testament, we had to keep those commandments because they were pleasing to God. If someone sinned, he or she must bring an animal (sheep or goat) to the Levitical priests who would make a sacrificial offering to cover our sin. It did not erase the sin or cleanse it but it covered it until the Messiah would come.

Faith in Jesus blood shed for us, washes us clean. God erases the sin as if it did not exist. This is the core of the New Covenant. It is believing in Jesus Christ as our Saviour and accepting the blessings and the responsibilities associated with it. There are two types of sins associated with all humans: original sin because we were born in the human race and Adam and Eve our ancestors sinned against God and we inherit that sin nature from them. Also, there is actual sin. Sin is willfully disobeying God and breaking one or more of the commandments.

Water Baptism not just an Outward sign

Water baptism, like all sacraments, is not just an outward sign of our faith. It has two parts to it: the outward sign and the inner spiritual working. It is a holy action when it is done with faith. Without faith, it is simply getting wet. With faith, it can have deep significance in the life of a believer.

A believer enters into water baptism with repentance. The believer knows that he or she could never be pleasing to God without the blood of Jesus Christ. It is in full obedience to a life of Christian dedication to God. The participant is making a vow to serve God for the rest of his or her life. It is symbolically and significantly identification with Jesus death, burial and resurrection. The Word Baptismo (Greek) means to be totally immersed in the water. The person should be totally immersed in water. John the Baptist was baptizing people who repented and turned towards God. The disciples of Jesus Baptized also.

Romans 6: 4 We were therefore buried with him through baptism into death in order that, just as Christ was raised from the dead through the glory of the Father, we too may live a new life.

Colossians 2: 12 having been buried with him in baptism, in which you were also raised with him through your faith in the working of God, who raised him from the dead.

In water baptism, a spiritual change can occur in the person. It can radically transform a person's life. If it were only an outward sign, Jesus would not command us to do it.

Mark 16: 15 He said to them, "Go into all the world and preach the gospel to all creation. 16 Whoever believes and is baptized will be saved, but whoever does not believe will be condemned. 17 And these signs will accompany those who believe: In my name, they will drive out demons; they will speak in new tongues; 18 they will pick up snakes with their hands;

and when they drink deadly poison, it will not hurt them at all; they will place their hands on sick people, and they will get well."

Jesus clearly commanded his disciples to preach the good news but also to water baptize people.

Jesus told Nicodemus that a man must be born of spirit and of water. Being born of water can be our natural birth, but is more than it. It can mean the washing of the water of the Word (Ephesians 5: 26) of God but it also means water baptism.

John 3: 5 Jesus answered, "Very truly I tell you, no one can enter the kingdom of God unless they are born of water and the Spirit.

Believers' Baptism

Believers in Jesus Christ as Saviour should be water baptism. If you do not believe you should not be water baptized. I am preaching a believer's baptism. Although it is proper to bless the children and pray a dedicatory prayer over them, they are not yet believers in Jesus. Believers who with their own free will choose to live for Jesus Christ, should take the next step which is to obey and become water baptized.

Acts 2: 38 Peter replied, "Repent and be baptized, every one of you, in the name of Jesus Christ for the forgiveness of your sins. And you will receive the gift of the Holy Spirit. 39 The promise is for you and your children and for all who are far off—for all whom the Lord our God will call."

There is an association with water baptism and repentance and believing in Jesus Christ and there is an association with the Holy Spirit. Before you had the revelation that Jesus was your Saviour, you were a sinner. You enjoyed sinning and couldn't help yourself. Once you receive Jesus as Saviour, Jesus washes us and cleanses us. Obedience in water baptism is a promise of your life to live for God. Please don't fall for the lie that you must be perfect to be water baptized. Only Jesus is Holy. His blood makes us holy. In ourselves we can do nothing, but Jesus Christ who lives in us, in the person of the Holy Spirit teaches us, convicts us, strengthens us and empowers us to live for Christ.

Hebrews 2: 10 In bringing many sons and daughters to glory, it was fitting that God, for whom and through whom everything exists, should make the pioneer of their salvation perfect through what he suffered. 11 Both the one who makes people holy and those who are made holy are of the same

Chris A. Legebow

family. So Jesus is not ashamed to call them brothers and sisters.

God is able to keep us from falling. The same mighty God who cleanses us is also able to keep us from falling. His righteousness imparted into us makes us holy and blameless. You don't have to believe that you can live holy. That is the main reason many people do not get water baptized. They say to themselves, I don't believe I can live holy to God. Your faith should be that Jesus Christ living in you is able to keep you holy and your faith should be in the shed blood of Jesus Christ to keep you – not in your own strength. No person could in his or her own strength live holy. The good news is that we don't have to do it in our own strength. We can live Holy because God lives on the inside of us and can keep us.

Philippians 4: 13 I can do all this through him who gives me strength.

Baptized

In some places in scripture is tells us to be baptized in the name of the Father, the Son and the Holy Spirit. In other places, it commands us to be baptized in the name of Jesus. Jesus Christ is LORD. I literally mean the words I've stated. Jesus, our Saviour, the Son of God who was born of a virgin, suffered, died and rose again. Christ is the Greek word for the Anointed One. The Holy Spirit is in Jesus without measure. That means He is fully and completely filled with the Holy Spirit. LORD is the tetragrammaton (JHWH) that we translate as Jehovah or LORD – meaning all God the creator and "I AM that I AM". Jesus Christ is LORD. He is one with God and equal to God.

Matthew 28: 19 Therefore go and make disciples of all nations, baptizing them in the name of the Father and of the Son and of the Holy Spirit, 20 and teaching them to obey everything I have commanded you. And surely I am with you always, to the very end of the age."

Acts 19: 5 On hearing this, they were baptized in the name of the Lord Jesus. 6 When Paul placed his hands on them, the Holy Spirit came on them, and they spoke in tongues[b] and prophesied. 7 There were about twelve men in all.

There are strong feelings about these simple truths I mentioned. Some would be outraged that we did not follow the teachings of Matthew 28. Others would be outraged that we did not follow the teachings of Acts 19. Please if this is a cause of offense for you, repent and be baptized in either one so that you may receive the Holy Spirit.

Romans 6: 3 Or don't you know that all of us who were baptized into Christ Jesus were baptized into his death? 4 We were therefore buried with him through baptism into death in order that, just as Christ was raised from the dead through the glory of the Father, we too may live a new life.

This scripture is not only a nice analogy. It is a symbolic but spiritually significant thing that occurs. As you go under the waters, you are baptized into Jesus death and burial; as you rise up out of the waters, you are rising to newness of life in Christ as He arose from the dead.

It should be taught with this understanding to those who are getting baptized. It is our faith in the scriptures and in Jesus death, burial and resurrection that give us spiritual strength. The engrafted scripture can transform your life completely (James 1: 21). As you come up out of the water, you are raised to newness of life. If we truly believe in what Jesus did for us, we can completely believe in this transformation of ourselves in water baptism. It is a spiritual thing. You are committing your life to Jesus Christ as a believer. Yes; there is an outward sign. Usually, believers are baptized in front of the church. They are witnessing your step of faith. It is not necessary though, remember how Philip preached that Jesus is the Messiah to the Ethiopian Eunuch and he was baptized by the side of the road (Acts 8: 27).

The inner work of God

Also, though, there is the part of water baptism that is between you and God. That is the inner working of God in your life. Your faith in Jesus as Saviour is expressed. If you will believer for Jesus the deliverer to circumcise your heart, you will receive it.

Acts 2: 29 No, a person is a Jew who is one inwardly; and circumcision is circumcision of the heart, by the Spirit, not by the written code. Such a person's praise is not from other people, but from God.

God promised that He would bring a New Covenant to Israel. He promised to soften their hearts.

Jeremiah 31: 33

33 But this shall be the covenant that I will make with the house of Israel
   after those days, says the Lord:
I will put My law within them

and write it in their hearts;
and I will be their God,
and they shall be My people.

Ezekiel 36: 26 Also, I will give you a new heart, and a new spirit I will put within you. And I will take away the stony heart out of your flesh, and I will give you a heart of flesh. 27 I will put My Spirit within you and cause you to walk in My statutes, and you will keep My judgments and do them.

A spiritual work is done on our heart when we enter into water baptism by faith. Enmity or hatred towards God is cut out. The hard spot you never let God in, becomes soft and you wholly want God with all your spirit, soul and body (1 Thessalonians 5: 23). The only way enmity can be cut out of your heart is by faith in Jesus Christ. It can occur in the waters of baptism should you know that it can. The old sinful nature can be cut off and new spiritual life blossom in that area of your life. If you do not believe for it, it will not happen.

Your hardiness of heart can be cut out and it can be replaced with a soft heart or passionate heart for God.

Hebrews 10: 15 The Holy Spirit also testifies to us about this. First he says:

16 "This is the covenant I will make with them
    after that time, says the Lord.
I will put my laws in their hearts,
    and I will write them on their minds."[b]

17 Then he adds:

"Their sins and lawless acts
    I will remember no more."[c]

18 And where these have been forgiven, sacrifice for sin is no longer necessary.

He promised to cut out their hard hearts or the enmity or hatred they had towards God. A person is born in sin because of Adam and Eve's transgression or sin against God. Every person born on earth has this sin nature. It must die so if we are to live in the Spirit. Also, people who sin and keep sinning, get hardened to that sin. They might feel guilt at first, but if they sin and keep sinning that sin. They get hardened like a callous on your hand or foot. That means the hard spot blocks God from that place in their lives.

Oh, please realize it is most serious. Just because they feel no remorse does not mean they are no sinning. I will compare it to this example.
Leprosy, is a horrible disease. We usually don't see it in North America, but it still exists in some places of the world without a cure. People can treat you but there is no known cure. The most dangerous aspect of the disease is that it kills nerves so that the people can't feel pain anymore. They could touch a hot stove and not know it. Please see, the chances of real damage to the person can occur because the people don't even know it is a danger. God promised to send us hope from being hard hearted in sin.

Jeremiah 31: 33 "This is the covenant I will make with the people of Israel
    after that time," declares the Lord.
"I will put my law in their minds
    and write it on their hearts.
I will be their God,
    and they will be my people.
34 No longer will they teach their neighbor,
    or say to one another, 'Know the Lord,'
because they will all know me,
    from the least of them to the greatest,"
declares the Lord.
"For I will forgive their wickedness
    and will remember their sins no more."

God promised to transform us so that we would not be the same. A person can be baptized in faith believing for circumcision of heart – that means expecting that any part of you that needs to die because it is hard against God – will die. Just as in the covenant with Abraham, all males had to be circumcised, as a sign of their faith in the covenant, God Himself circumcises our inner hearts of any hardness towards God. It includes original sin (inherited from Adam and Eve) but also any hardness of heart that comes through inherited sins or iniquities.

Iniquity

Iniquity is inherited sins that are passed through the bloodline of a family. What it means is that certain family all commit similar sins. It can be passed on for generations.

Numbers 14: 18 'The Lord is slow to anger, abounding in love and forgiving sin and rebellion. Yet he does not leave the guilty unpunished; he punishes the children for the sin of the parents to the third and fourth generation.'

Inherited sins or iniquities

You may see that diseases may run in certain families. There are things that can be genetically inherited. Similarly, certain sins, are spiritually inherited, until someone repents and prays mercy for his or her family and all the generations to follow. After you are saved and have repented for your sins, you should pray for the Holy Spirit to quicken to you any iniquities in your family. By the gift of discerning of spirits, God can show you the iniquities. You can repent of them and pray for your family to be delivered from their sins. Only God Himself can set them free. Your prayers, can release people who could share Christ with them. Your prayers could release angels who will intervene and protect them. I have known of parents who get an anointed cloth from the prayer meeting praying deliverance for a loved one, who place that cloth in the loved one's room. It is the faith that makes the difference.

If you are not yet water Baptized

If you are a Christian but you have not been water baptized, I want you to examine your heart as to why. It is not a normal thing to hesitate to obey God once you know His commandments. Hesitation means there is an issue. Jesus commanded us to teach and preach water baptism. This means we should want to obey Jesus Christ and follow. Don't let any lie of the enemy tell you that you aren't good enough to be water baptized. That is a lie from the devil. Jesus blood makes you holy. All aspects of our Christian faith are focused on the Holiness of Jesus Christ and what He did for us. It's not what we can do for Him or what we can give Him. Our best efforts are nowhere near God's standard for complete holiness. Only Jesus is our hope of righteousness.

Romans 2: 22 This righteousness is given through faith in[h] Jesus Christ to all who believe. There is no difference between Jew and Gentile,

1 Corinthians 5: 21 God made him who had no sin to be sin[b] for us, so that in him we might become the righteousness of God.

If you are hesitating to be water baptized, and it is not that you don't believe that Jesus is your righteousness, and you don't even know the reason why but you just can't commit to water baptism, I would highly recommend fasting and prayer. It can be your choice, partial fast or liquid fast, but you should seek God and ask Him to show you why you are hesitating. There may be some part of your life that you must submit to God.

I was baptized as a baby

My parents were not Christians, but it was the thing people did. I have no memory of it at all. I was prayed for and sprinkled with water as a baby. Believe me I had no confession of faith in Jesus. I couldn't even walk without holding on to things. I've seen the pictures of me all dressed up in the prettiest dress, holding on to furniture as I walked around the living room. If you were baptized as a baby, you should meditate on whether or not you should be water baptized for a believers' baptism – immersed in water.

In no way does this insult your parents. They did what they thought was best, but you really had no say about it. The truth is now you do. The Bible clearly teaches immersion baptism for believers.

The reason some churches sprinkle water baptize comes from the early church in Rome who were persecuted for their faith if they worshipped openly. They used the minimum requirement of drops of water rather than immersion because they could not openly water baptize in public places. A sprinkle of water would represent what was meant to be total immersion. I believe God has much mercy on Christians who can no openly confess their faith, but we in North America have no reason not to be baptized in water. We should not be satisfied with the minimum requirement because of tradition rather than what the Bible states we are to do.

The Waters of baptism do not make you holy

The outward action of being baptized has no significance if you have no faith. You must believe in Jesus for there to be any significance. Some people believe the sacraments themselves are what makes you holy but it is not scriptural. Faith in Jesus Christ makes you holy. Obedience to God makes you a scriptural Christian.

God knows we humans need some profound significant aspects of our faith (outward signs) to make the inner working of the Holy Spirit more memorable for us. The sacraments are memorial markers in our Christian faith. They are important. We celebrate them. We respect them. We should treasure them. We should teach them to our children so they understand the significance even while they are children.

Identification with Jesus

You should not enter in to any sacrament without instruction. You should get some teaching from your parents, or from someone at your church. Sometimes it is taught in a classroom or sometimes it is taught by ministers the day of the sacrament. Getting spiritual instruction as well as practical instruction helps the process to go smoothly.

Think of it as being immersed in Jesus: His death, burial and resurrection. Identify with it and believe that as you partake in it, it will affect your life. You are completely one with Jesus. You are in Christ and Christ is in you. You are stating, my life is hid in Christ. I am one with Jesus in death, burial and resurrection. Jesus is the only holiness for me.

Colossians 3: 3 For you died, and your life is now hidden with Christ in God. 4 When Christ, who is your[a] life, appears, then you also will appear with him in glory.

Romans 6: 3 Or don't you know that all of us who were baptized into Christ Jesus were baptized into his death? 4 We were therefore buried with him through baptism into death in order that, just as Christ was raised from the dead through the glory of the Father, we too may live a new life.

The identification is literal. You believe in your heart that Christ died for you but you also enter in by demonstrating your faith through obedience to God and are immersed in water – into the death, burial and resurrection of Jesus Christ. The identification places you as a participant rather than an observer. Rather than stand at the foot of the cross to see Jesus dying for your sins, you believe you are in Christ – His death replaces your own death. Surely the sentence of sin is death and you and I are worthy of death because of it. You are in Christ – with Him as He died on that cross, as He defeated hell and the grave, as He rose to newness of life. You are in Christ – He is seated on the Throne in heaven: He prays for you as well as answers your prayers.

Fruit of the Spirit

Although we are in complete identification with Christ in baptism, the character of Christ is formed in us as we are changed from glory to glory in the presence of God in prayer and in reading of God's Word. Usually, water baptism is a place of deciding for more of God and pressing into Christ more than ever before. What that means is the person will want to hear preaching, desire to read God's word and pray, seek God and spiritual friends more than in the past. These decisions all focus on Jesus Christ and what occurs is Christ's character begins to be formed in your inner most being.

Galatians 5: 22 But the fruit of the Spirit is love, joy, peace, forbearance, kindness, goodness, faithfulness, 23 gentleness and self-control. Against such things there is no law.

What happens with the believer who dedicates his or her life to God is that he or she becomes more like God the more you are in God's presence. The characteristics we would use to describe Christ will be formed in us. Generally, it includes all the fruit of the Spirit and also these qualities: merciful, kind, compassionate, caring, forgiving, giving, generous, genuine. You may not notice it in yourself but others will see it in you. They may comment.

Occasionally upon self-reflection, you will think of how God has changed you so that the way you used to be either angry or put off, you will now be kind and patient and forgiving. What is occurring is very special. The Holy Spirit is making you more like Christ so that your life can give God glory. People will see Christ in you. They may ask you about God because of it or perhaps you will have an opportunity to witness to someone because they will ask you why you are so positive.

Because Jesus is living on the inside of you, and because you are desiring to know more of God, the fruit of the Spirit is more evident in your life. Part of it is you don't do the same things you did before you knew Christ. Part of it is you don't think the way you did before you knew Christ. Your spirit has been born- again. The Holy Spirit's presence in you makes all the difference.

2 Peter 1: 3 His divine power has given us everything we need for a godly life through our knowledge of him who called us by his own glory and goodness. 4 Through these he has given us his very great and precious promises, so that through them you may participate in the divine nature, having escaped the corruption in the world caused by evil desires.
5 For this very reason, make every effort to add to your faith goodness; and to goodness, knowledge; 6 and to knowledge, self-control; and to self-control, perseverance; and to perseverance, godliness; 7 and to godliness, mutual affection; and to mutual affection, love. 8 For if you possess these qualities in increasing measure, they will keep you from being ineffective

and unproductive in your knowledge of our Lord Jesus Christ. 9 But whoever does not have them is nearsighted and blind, forgetting that they have been cleansed from their past sins.

God gives us all things for a godly life, but we should be making every effort to add to our faith. The Holy Spirit living in us is changing us but we also should be sensitive to the Holy Spirit and we should add to our faith. It is not as though we could do it without God's help. Literally, it means that God will shine the light on areas of our lives and we will pray concerning these things and get the Word of God on the inside of us by reading it, praying it, and confessing it.

Peace, that passes all understanding, joy, and His godly nature. I read an excellent book by Thomas A Kempis right after I got saved called "The Imitation of Christ". It is a book about being transformed by God to become more Christ like. It is an excellent book, but not everyone may like the early English because it is about a thousand years old. This early saint of the Christian Church had a revelation of what it means to identify with Christ. It means that is Christ is, so should we be.

Philippians 2: 5 In your relationships with one another, have the same mindset as Christ Jesus:
Who, being in very nature[a] God,
    did not consider equality with God something to be used to his own advantage;
7 rather, he made himself nothing
    by taking the very nature[b] of a servant,
    being made in human likeness.
8 And being found in appearance as a man,
    he humbled himself
    by becoming obedient to death—
        even death on a cross!

Serving

This scripture tells us that we should be made like Christ in our desire to serve. We should enjoy serving and helping others. It should become a part of our character. We should desire to serve God by sharing Christ with others. We should care about people and be quick to give help to people. Because you are a part of the body of Christ, God will speak to you and prompt you to pray for people or to help people. God will place someone on your heart and you will check on that person and encourage him or her and make a difference.

The love you have for people will be clear because you will start caring about people at church in a new way. You may pray for them more or listen to them more because you really care. It will also include non-Christians. Our love for people should be so strong that it compels us to share Jesus Christ with them. They will see something different about us rather than other people. They will see something of Christ in us causing us to make a difference. Our lives should be so radical that Christ living in us lives through us.

We do not do things because we have to, we do them because we wat to – we want to show God's love for people. We want to make a difference in our community. We want people to get saved. We want to help people if all we do is plant a seed of faith in them. Because we know the goodness of Christ, we will want to share it with others. Should you speak to someone for five or six minutes, you will hear the most important things in that person's life. Listening to them and responding with caring will make the biggest difference. What we do in faith is honoured by God.

Hebrews 11: 6 And without faith it is impossible to please God, because anyone who comes to him must believe that he exists and that he rewards those who earnestly seek him

5 THE BAPTISM OF THE HOLY SPIRIT

Chapter 5

The Baptism of the Holy Spirit

Should you go to a full gospel church or a Church that preaches the gifts of the Holy Spirit in the Church today, you will hopefully see evidence of the Baptism of the Holy Spirit within your first several services at the Church. The evidence of the Baptism of the Holy Spirit most usual is the speaking in other tongues or praising God in other tongues. Sometimes, there will be dancing; sometimes there will be weeping with gratitude to God; sometimes, people will be slain in the Spirit (fall to the ground and tremble). It is the presence of the Holy Spirit so strong that a human body can hardly contain it. The Baptism of the Holy Spirit is the overwhelming presence of God filling a Christian so that Jesus Christ Himself immerses that believer in the Holy Spirit.

How you might receive it

You can receive the Baptism of the Holy Spirit in several ways. The easiest way is to know about it, pray to receive the gift because it is promised to all believers in Jesus Christ. You could have a Christian friend or minister lay hands on you and pray for you that you might receive the baptism of the Holy Spirit I will give my own testimony later: it is the other way which is by a sovereign move of God.

The Baptism of the Holy Spirit is for all who are Christians

Acts 2: 38 Peter said to them, "Repent and be baptized, every one of you, in the name of Jesus Christ for the forgiveness of sins, and you shall receive the gift of the Holy Spirit. 39 For the promise is to you, and to your children, and to all who are far away, as many as the Lord our God will call."

Jesus promised to give it so that the disciples would be comforted and so that they would be empowered to preach Jesus Christ to all the earth. It was promised by Jesus. It was manifested on earth at the feast of Pentecost in Acts 2. It is the presence of God, both the fruit of the spirit and the gifts of God are quickened by the baptism of the Holy Spirit making the believer more excellent at ministering and witnessing.

John 14: 16 I will pray the Father, and He will give you another Counselor, that He may be with you forever:

Luke 24: 49 And look, I am sending the promise of My Father upon you. But wait in the city of Jerusalem until you are clothed with power from on high."

Mark 16: 15 He said to them, "Go into all the world, and preach the gospel to every creature. 16 He who believes and is baptized will be saved. But he who does not believe will be condemned. 17 These signs will accompany those who believe: In My name they will cast out demons; they will speak with new tongues; 18 they will take up serpents; if they drink any deadly thing, it will not hurt them; they will lay hands on the sick, and they will recover."

Prayer Language

The Baptism of the Holy Spirit is not simply something a Christian does once or every once in a while. It would be neglecting an important part of our life with God. The baptism of the Holy Spirit with the speaking in other tongues is an essential aspect of communing with God. We can use our prayer language to pray for ourselves, others, nations etc. It is God literally praying in us and through us, the perfect will of God for the thing we are praying about.

Romans 8: 26 Likewise, the Spirit helps us in our weaknesses, for we do not know what to pray for as we ought, but the Spirit Himself intercedes for us with groanings too deep for words. 27 He who searches the hearts knows what the mind of the Spirit is, because He intercedes for the saints according to the will of God.

PRAYING IN TONGUES Taken from my book on prayer

The good news is that if you have not been baptized in the Holy Spirit speaking in other tongues – you can be. You must believe that Jesus is your Saviour – you must pray in faith believing that the gift of the baptism of the Holy Spirit with the evidence of speaking in tongues is for today. What happens is that you press in as close as you can get to God wanting more of Him and He fills you to overflowing with His Spirit. You may shake or tremble; you may be slain in the spirit (fall down); you may start crying or laughing; you may simply continue praising God from English and you hear the words to speak in a different language and start doing it.

As you were baptized or immersed in water for water baptism, so are you immersed in the Holy Spirit in the Baptism of the Holy Spirit. You will begin to speak in languages you have never learned. There are two types of this expression: one is praying in an unknown language only known by God. Sometimes God will reveal to you what you are saying. The origin is the Holy Spirit. This gift is used in the church sometimes.

The second expression is similar, you are speaking in a language you haven't learned but it is a language of the earth, of a different people. This was the use on the day of Pentecost as the 120 were gathered in the upper room were filled with the Spirit, immersed in the Spirit so strongly that they were compelled to go into the streets praising and worshipping God in these new languages. (Acts 2) The pilgrims were gathered to celebrate Pentecost and they heard the 120 praising God in their own languages from different regions and nations.

You can be baptized in the Holy Spirit by praying for it. It is a gift of God and so you should desire it. You may ask God for it and He can fill you to overflowing. You may receive it by pressing into God and wanting more of Him. You may not even know what has happened to you. That is what happened to me as a new Christian.

My own testimony

I had been saved for approximately 2 or 3 months. I had no Bible teaching – only preaching from the pulpit. I was not from a Christian home. Every service I attended, I felt drawn to go pray at the altar. I prayed and praised God that day. The Minister speaking was visiting and was asking people to commit their lives to live for Christ all their lives.

He let us know it was serious and might mean going to be a missionary or to do anything God prompted us to do. I felt the tugging of God at my heart so strong, I nearly ran to the altar area. There were thousands of people there – you couldn't get close to the platform. I committed myself wholly to follow the LORD asking for all of Him, praying to know Him more, desiring more of Him. I was worshipping God and surrendering my life to Him as I started speaking in a different language I didn't know. It wasn't scary – it was unique. My friend was standing near to me and it scared her so she left me there. I was oblivious to all other surroundings – I was fixed on seeking God and worshipping Him.

I mentioned what happened to the friend who lead me to Christ and she explained to me what it was. Please know I was a new Christian, not yet baptized in water but wholly desiring God; God mercifully baptized me in the Holy Spirit.

The Presence of God

Most people who experience this will say they have felt the presence of the LORD very strong; they were filled with peace; they were worshipping to overflowing. This means you worship and you worship and you worship and all you want to do is stay in the presence of God. It is hard to find natural words to describe what spiritually occurs. Literally, it is God Himself filling us with Himself so that we are flowing in the Holy Spirit with our spirit. I would describe it as a fountain that is flowing with the well-spring of water deeply within you; there is no ending to the glory that keeps bubbling up. Jesus said (John 4) that He would give us water that would never stop flowing.

Let's look here in Acts 2: 1- 4. It describes the way the disciples were baptized in the Holy Spirit.

Acts 2: 1 When the day of Pentecost had come, they were all together in one place. 2 Suddenly a sound like a mighty rushing wind came from heaven, and it filled the whole house where they were sitting. 3 There appeared to them tongues as of fire, being distributed and resting on each of them, 4 and they were all filled with the Holy Spirit and began to speak in other tongues, as the Spirit enabled them to speak.

The Disciples Who Received the Baptism of the Holy Spirit

These disciples had witnessed Jesus Resurrected from the dead. Many of them saw Him visibly ascend into heaven surrounded by angels. Jesus instructed them to wait in Jerusalem for the gift of the Holy Spirit. They obeyed and gathered in the upper room praying for what Jesus promised; the Spirit of God was poured on them. This occasion was unique and I know of no other occasion in scripture or in testimony where little tongues of fire – or lamps of fire were evident above people's heads. It occurred that day so they could see it. It was the fulfillment of the promise of the gift of the Spirit (Joel 2) that would empower them to preach and teach Christ so that all people could know that Jesus is the Saviour of all people.

I have heard of instances with the outpouring of the spirit where people saw a supernatural glow or light or radiance – but not exactly the same as on the day of Pentecost. It was a sign to the believing Jews who gathered at Pentecost; it was a sign to the disciple themselves that God had fulfilled His promise and it was a sign to us who read God's Word that we might know our God is mighty and desires to pour His Spirit upon us even though we are living in temporal bodies. I would compare this event in importance to God appearing to Moses in the burning bush. It radically changed the nations.

Your first speaking in tongues may be compared to a baby who is learning his or her natural language. There may be syllables; there may be phrases; there might not be a full flow. To some people, it's like a gusher, a fountain springing in full use; others, it starts slowly as you yield to the Holy Spirit. The more you pray in tongues, the smoother the flow will be. You may have recurring phrases that God gives to you especially. It is like a natural language because there are words, phrases etc.

The Groanings of the Spirit

The gift of tongues is not simply for feeling the presence of God. Please let me add, if that were the only benefit, I would desire it so strongly anyway. But there is an impartation of God's Spirit filling our human spirit so that we are praying the perfect will of God.

Romans 8: 26 Likewise, the Spirit helps us in our weaknesses, for we do not know what to pray for as we ought, but the Spirit Himself intercedes for us with groanings too deep for words. 27 He who searches the hearts knows what the mind of the Spirit is, because He intercedes for the saints according to the will of God.

Please understand this. I am saying that the Holy Spirit living inside us – fills us to overflowing so that we start praying the perfect will of God for ourselves or others. The groanings of the Spirit lead us to pray – we may not always know what we are praying for; sometimes though God reveals to us an interpretation of the tongue or words of knowledge about the tongue we are speaking.

On the day of Pentecost, the 120 were praising God and went out into the streets of Jerusalem praising God in their new tongues. Over 2, 000 people got saved. People from other nations, heard God being praised in their own language by men who were fishermen not scholars. Peter preaches a sermon about Jesus as Messiah and his death, burial and resurrection. The people respond with faith and the church is multiplied exponentially because of the Baptism of the Holy Spirit.

A Sign to Those who Want to Know God

The Baptism of the Holy Spirit empowers us to preach or teach Christ. The gifts of the Spirit help us to build up the body of Christ. The fruit of the Spirit makes our lives living examples of God's character in the earth. The early church multiplied at a rapid rate.

As it was in the book of Acts, so it is today. The manifest out pouring of the Holy Spirit in the church causes people to want to be there. Most people will know it is wondrous and desire to know more. We should not be trying to spare the visitors from the gifts of the Spirit. The gifts of the Spirit will attract people and cause them to want to know God. They are given to us so that we could minister. The church will multiply if the gifts of the Spirit are in the church. The Lord will add to the church as we pursue Him.

1 Corinthians 12: 4 There are various gifts, but the same Spirit. 5 There are differences of administrations, but the same Lord. 6 There are various operations, but it is the same God who operates all of them in all people.7 But the manifestation of the Spirit is given to everyone for the common good. 8 To one is given by the Spirit the word of wisdom, to another the word of knowledge by the same Spirit, 9 to another faith by the same Spirit, to another gifts of healings by the same Spirit, 10 to another the working of miracles, to another prophecy, to another discerning of spirits, to another various kinds of tongues, and to another the interpretation of tongues. 11 But that one and very same Spirit works all these, dividing to each one individually as He will.

Somebody baptized in the Holy Spirit, who is praying in the Spirit (praying in tongues earnestly) is someone God can use in divergent ways. You may be praying about something that will occur in your day and give you grace or cause you to assist someone in need. God can give you words or phrases in the interpretation of tongues that you may share with someone or that will encourage you. And you praise and pray in tongues, the other gifts of the Holy Spirit are released with fresh strength. You will feel compelled to give or serve, or teach or encourage or prophesy. The gifts are evidence of the Spirit living on the inside of you.

Each Christian has gifts and talents that God has given them; the Baptism of the Holy Spirit releases these people to minister in the body of Christ and also in the world they live in. God can use you to impact your community; your school; your workplace; your home; your family; all spheres of society – wherever you go, God can use you to be a witness of

His glory, His mercy and His compassion.

Life in the Spirit

The Holy Spirit is the medium that God uses to do spiritual activity on earth. For instance, I am typing this message; I could speak or preach this message; I could do a live session in front of people or I could tape it and record a DVD. Those are all mediums for the message on prayer that I am sharing, In this instance, my book, is the medium I am using. In the same way, God uses the Holy Spirit to do spiritual things on the earth through us. If there is a demand on the gift, and we are living in the Spirit, the Spirit will manifest the gift and the person will receive the answer to his or her faith. It usually results in miracles, healings, lives transformed.

I Would that you All Prophesy

1 Corinthians 14: 5 I desire that you all speak in tongues, but even more that you prophesy. For greater is he who prophesies than he who speaks in tongues, unless he interprets, so that the church may receive edification.

The Apostle Paul is the author who gives us church order. We who are Christians get our order of service from the Apostle Paul and the early Church. Paul is saying he wishes they all spoke in other tongues. There must be a reason for it. Usually, this verse is used only to emphasize – that even more so you would prophesy but I am saying if it wasn't important Paul wouldn't say he wanted them all to do it. The gift is for all people not only some. Whoever wants the gift and asks God for it, will receive it.

1 Corinthians 14: 18 I thank my God that I speak in tongues more than you all. 19 Yet in the church I had rather speak five words with my understanding, that by my voice I might teach others also, than ten thousand words in an unknown tongue.

There are places God uses us in our gifts: in our homes (in private) and in public in the church or in the marketplace your spheres of influence on the earth. God often deals with us in private as we are praising or praying in tongues and gives us revelation or insight into our day.

Although your first utterances in tongues may be simple syllables or words or phrases likened to a baby uttering his or her first words, we are not made to stay in an infant stage of tongues. As we use the gift of tongues to worship or praise or pray, our prayer language will develop as a steady flow. We will utter what the Spirit brings to us and we will get boldness knowing it is God speaking through us or praying through us. We will not get the full benefit of tongues if we do not use the gift often. It is meant for us to use regularly, so much that the Apostle Paul says I thank God that I pray in tongues more than you all. (1 Corinthians 14: 18) He is letting us know this gift is very important.

The Gift of Tongues in the Church Service

It is true Paul says the gift of prophecy should be desired so that we might build up the church, but that does not take away from the importance of using the gift of tongues. Sometimes in a service, someone will profoundly feel to give an utterance in tongues. What will usually happen is that person or another person will pray for the interpretation and speak it to the church afterwards. A different person might get the revelation of the interpretation and speak it out. If it is not right away, the pastor will often ask the congregation to pray for an interpretation. That is the proper use of the gift of tongues used in a church service.

By yourself though, you can be praying in tongues and knowing God is using you. If you feel a desire to know what you are praying, as you are praying in tongues also ask God to give you understanding of the matter. He will give it to you. It is not for anyone but yourself to know how the spirit is praying through you.

Place for Praying in Tongues in the Church

Standing at your seat or at the alter praying, as you yield to the Holy Spirit praying and praising in tongues, it quickens the other gifts of the Spirit. The gift of faith, gift of working of miracles, gift or prophecy etc. begin to be released and we may start ministering to those around us or feel a strong desire to do so. This is how the body of Christ was created – so that each part builds up the other parts. As you are flowing the in Holy Spirit, you will desire to impart something to those around you. If we did this in our churches – pray in the Spirit as a Church, pray in the Spirit at the altar, the gifts of the spirit would be manifest in our churches.

Oh it is good to praise the LORD and pray with understanding in the language that you speak, but there is a place of congregational prayer in tongues and ministry to people at the altar with tongues. This directly connects you to the giftings of God. If you are praying for somebody but you don't know what to say, start praying in tongues; God will move upon you with wisdom, words of wisdom, words of knowledge and discerning of spirits.

Special Holy Spirit Lead Worship in Tongues

Sometimes with an anointed prophetic worship leader, a song of the LORD may rise, praising God in tongues and with understanding. I've been in strong meetings where all the church will start worshipping in tongues and a new song in understanding will come forth and all the congregation will be singing the song the LORD has given the worship leader. This type of Holy Spirit lead atmosphere will be conductive to all sorts of gifts being activated and some people being instantly healed or set free. The gift of tongues and praising and worship in tongues is not for no reason – it releases faith, the manifest presence of God and the giftings within believers.

Apostolic Anointing

A special faith is released during these spiritual meetings and if an Apostle of God is leading, special faith and special miracles will be released in the service. Often the Apostle will be able to discern what should occur whether it is a special word of knowledge for the congregation or scriptures or a call for healing or a Jericho march around the church. The Apostle's direction will help to manifest God's will for that service and that congregation.

I would compare it to this. I have been in the Toronto train station on many occasions. I know it well. Should I see a picture of it or should I be there, I know my way around because I have been there so often. If suddenly I were transported into the midst of the Toronto train station, I would know exactly where I was – even though it would be weird – I would notice the familiar because I know the place.

The Apostle is much like this in the realms of the spirit because the Apostle is someone who presses into the Spirit and lives in the realms of God's glory. He or she, can spiritually discern the moving of the Holy Spirit and perceive what God wants to do in the service. How does he or she know? Because the Apostle lives in the realm of the spirit and is given authority to use in the congregation to lead and guide the congregation and to release the giftings in the Prophet, Pastor, Teacher and Evangelist. The gifts of the spirit are released as faith is released in believers' hearts.

During these types of meetings, people will repent without anyone asking them to. People will start crying; people will be healed physically. People may receive forgiveness. People may decide to become missionaries.

People may be set free from smoking or drinking or drugs. People will feel the presence of God and want to get right with God. Spirit manifest spirit. As you are praising and worshipping or praying in tongues, God can manifest in whatever you have need of.

Ephesians 6: 18 Pray in the Spirit always with all kinds of prayer and supplication.

Stir up your own self in the spirit.

In your home, as you pray, make part of your prayer a stirring of the gifts of the Spirit. We are instructed to stir up spiritual gifts. (2 Timothy 1: 6) You do this by literally praying over yourself and saying " I stir up the gift of faith. Gift of faith spring up – come forth." You do that over yourself regularly with all the gifts, God will be using you at church or at home or in the marketplace. Roberts Liardon, a mighty preacher and church historian has an excellent teaching on this topic of stirring up your gifts. If you could get a chance to listen to it, I highly recommend it to you. You can pray over yourself in your natural language and you can pray over yourself in tongues.

The Gift of Tongues

God gives us the gifts but we must stir them up; we must use them. It is possible to be baptized in the Holy Spirit and not to use the gift. It is possible to have the gifts of God but not stir them. It is possible that you may ignore them or not use them. The Holy Spirit will never force you to speak in tongues or force you to use any spiritual gift. The Holy Spirit is our teacher, our helper; He will prompt us but God highly regards our human will and will never violate it. Praying in tongues and the baptism of the Holy Spirit is the miraculous realm. It is an empowering for the service of Christ. If you ever don't know how to pray for yourself or someone, literally start praying in tongues, believing God will show you what to pray.

Years ago, I heard Kenneth Hagin Senior preach and give a challenge. He challenged anyone who needed a miracle form God to pray in tongues 1 hour a day for 30 days. He said that if someone did this but didn't get answer to pray to write him. I took his challenge praying in tongues, more and more each day. I never wrote him. I knew a key to life in the Spirit had been revealed to me and that God was speaking to me more and using me more because I was pressing in to Him with all my being and praying in tongues every day.

Because I was praying in tongues, I began dreaming dreams, seeing visions, being directed to pray for people; God would use me more; I would go for a walk someone would be there – I would share Christ frequently with strangers. My life was given to prayer, praise and evangelism. I also would get supernatural words of wisdom and knowledge concerning my own self and those around me.

The Baptism of the Holy Spirit with speaking in other tongues is for ourselves, but it is also to build up the Church. It is to help prepare the Body of Christ for Christ's return. God wants to use you; give yourself to God wholly: spirit soul and body; expect God to use you. Praying in tongues requires you living in the Spirit and being led by the Spirit.

The Baptism of the Holy Spirit taken from my book on spiritual Gifts

The Baptism of the Holy Spirit is a gift in itself, but it is not for no reason. We use it because it is God's way of communicating with us surpassing or superseding our brain. I do mean it literally. God goes right to the spirit – to communicate with us as we are praying in the Holy Spirit. Often, if you continue to pray in tongues, He will translate it for you, not always, but almost always – so that your brain can understand it. What I am talking about is living in the spirit, becoming strong in the spirit so that you, the spiritual you, is stronger than the human will, mind or emotions, and stronger than your physical body.

You are living in a different realm – the high calling of God for your life – to live as a spiritual person, to live as a spiritual person. Soon after a person is baptized in the Holy Spirit, there should be some teaching on the gifts of the spirit. I'm not against teaching it before it occurs, but the person will benefit the most afterwards. If you do not know the gifts are there, you might not even know it is a gift. You could be already functioning in it, but without teaching, you may not know it is something you can grow in and use for God's glory.

For instance, I'll give you an example from scripture; Joseph who had dreams may not have known it was a gift from God. He spoke it so freely with his family; if he had known it was a special gift from God, he might have also prayed about it and asked God for wisdom concerning it. If you do not know, you should not; it's possible to share your most intimate revelations from God with those who will only laugh at you or hate you for it. God used images and visions to speak to him and give him prophetic insight as to what would happen in his life.

6 LAYING ON OF HANDS

Chapter 6

The laying on of Hands taken from my book on The Sacraments

Laying on of Hands

Hebrews 6: 1 Therefore, leaving the elementary principles of the doctrine of Christ, let us go on to maturity, not laying again a foundation of repentance from dead works and of faith toward God, 2 of instruction about washings, the laying on of hands, the resurrection of the dead, and eternal judgment.

In the foundation stones of the Christian faith, laying on of hands is named as an essential foundations. It is also a sacrament. Although it is often practiced in the Christian Church in most denominations, it is not always done with faith which means it is just an external action rather than a two-part sacrament. Whatever is not of faith cannot be considered sacred. It is impossible to please God without Faith.

The Laying on of Hands

The literal Biblical interpretation is that we Christians believe that as we place hands on someone and pray for him or her, a spiritual transaction occurs. There is a transference from spirit to spirit because of the Holy Spirit and the Holy faith to do so. The Holy Spirit anointing on a person can be transferred to a believer by placing hands on the person and prayer. Faith is imparted. Sometimes, healing is imparted; sometimes confirmation of truths learned is imparted. This does not mean that prayer without laying on of hands is not effective. Jesus layed hands on people and they were healed. In some situations, in scripture, the apostles layed their hands on people for any of the above reasons.

As the disciples preached Jesus Christ after Pentecost, they had boldness to preach the infilling of the Holy Spirit or the Baptism of the Holy Spirit. Sometimes, they simply prayed for the Spirit to come on a person, but in this instance as they shared about the Baptism of the Holy Spirit, they literally placed their hands on the believers in faith for the gift of the Holy Spirit to be given to these Samaritans

In Acts 8: 17 Then they laid their hands on them, and they received the Holy Spirit.

Often a common method that God uses to baptism someone in the Holy Spirit is that believers filled with the Holy Spirit lay hands in faith on those who want the gift. I mean a literal transference such as this example. I throw a ball to you and you catch it in your hands. Substance is transferred. The Holy Spirit within us anoints us to lay hands for a spiritual purpose; there is a transference of spirit to spirit. The effects may not be immediate or they may be. Usually, what occurs with baptism of the Holy Spirit is that a person begins to glorify God and as he or she does, tongues the person has never learned come up out of the innermost being of the person. It is an impartation of the Holy Spirit. Jesus Christ Himself is the Baptizer and uses a Spirit filled willing vessel to flow through the vessel to a person such as copper wiring is used as a conduit for the flow of current.

Also, spiritual gifts can be imparted by the laying on of hands. An example of this is Where Moses lays hands on Joshua according to the commandment of God.

Numbers 27: 18 The Lord said to Moses, "Take Joshua the son of Nun, a man in whom is the Spirit, and lay your hand on him, 19 and cause him to stand before Eleazar the priest and before all the assembly, and command in their sight. 20 You will put some of your majesty on him, in order that all the assembly of the children of Israel will listen. 21 He will stand before Eleazar the priest, who will ask for him about the judgment of the Urim before the Lord. At his word will they go out, and at his word they will come in, both he and all the children of Israel with him, even all the assembly."

It is God who instructs Moses on what to do. God explains the transference of spirit to spirit. God promises to impart some of the anointing of Moses onto Joshua. Moses prays for Joshua to have wisdom and strength to lead Israel. It is done publicly with the approval of the priests. It is not only a transference but it shows the people of Israel what God is doing. God clearly chooses the successor to Moses. Moses did not decide by himself. The people see the results of obedience to God. What it does is build their faith and trust in Joshua. The results are that all of Joshua`s life, the people of Israel followed God and obeyed Joshua as a leader of the people. They keep their promise to follow Joshua as they had followed Moses.

Joshua 1: 16 They answered Joshua, "All that you command us we will do, and wherever you send us we will go. 17 Just as we obeyed Moses in all things, we will obey you. May the Lord your God be with you, as He was with Moses! 18 Whoever rebels against your command and disobeys your words, in all that you command him, shall be put to death. Only be strong and courageous."

Joshua was not a stranger to the children of Israel. Joshua was close to Moses and was entrusted to help Moses. Joshua was mentored by Moses. The people of Israel knew him well. Moses, passes on gifts through the transference of spirit to spirit. The Bible says that a spirit of wisdom rested on Joshua because of it.

Barnabus and Saul

In this next instance, the disciples were praying and someone prophesied that Barnabus and Saul should be separated unto God for ministry.

Acts 13: 2 As they worshipped the Lord and fasted, the Holy Spirit said, "Set apart for Me Barnabas and Saul for the work to which I have called them." 3 Then after fasting and praying, they laid their hands on them and sent them off.

Clearly it is not symbolic. The disciples prayed and fasted and laid hands and prayed. They seriously considered the action as sacred or holy. It is not simply a rite or an outward sign. It has significance. It is not a ritual. It is an expression of faith and an action done in faith so that God may use humans as vessels that He can pour His glory through.

It is an awesome thing to be sent by a church to minster. I have been a part of several churches where people were prayed for, sometimes prophesied over, and sent into ministry as missionaries or released into specific ministries locally. I was a part of a church who often prayed over prayer teams who would go pray throughout the city as they walked and prayed and believed God would pour out his Spirit in that area. Sometimes, they would evangelize on the street. Sometimes they would go just before the evening movie was to start. They would pray for anyone in the long ups.

Sometimes, they would preach to those in the long lines ups to popular bars on a Friday or Saturday. Other times, they would walk and pray claiming souls. Literally, the church would be praying and the pastors and elders would lay hands on us and pray that God would use us to pray and evangelize so that Christ would be magnified. They prayed for success but also anointing us with their authority and the church's authority to accomplish what we were sent to do.

Ritual or Sacrament

A ritual is something people do but it doesn`t necessarily have any power to it. For instance, lighting a candle is something people do as part of worship in many denominations. Its meaning is symbolic only. It had meaning in the Old Testament because God instructed the priests to do it. Bowing one`s head to pray is also a ritual. Many people observe it. The Bible doesn`t say to bow your head and pray. The opposite is true. The Psalmist tells us to lift up our heads to praise God (Psalm 24: 9).

Laying on of hands is not just a religious rite. If you are only completing a ceremony with no faith – there is no sacrament only ritual. The difference between faith filled believers laying hands believing and imparting to believers and those just doing a ritual is huge. It is important that laying on of hands be practiced with faith because it is one of the fundamental doctrines of the Christian Church.

Don`t believe that the laying on of hands without faith will accomplish anything. Also, don`t elevate the laying on of hands of be something it is not. There are certain places it is used. It is not used for everything. Don't believe that you must receive by laying on of hands. It`s one way of receiving. I want to give an example of receiving by faith but still receiving.

Never be Religious

Religious to me means, it must be this way and God can`t do it any other way; I never want to be religious. God can use all kinds of ways to impart to people and to inspire or release people. Years ago, there was a special Evangelist who was preaching at my church during a youth convention. He would evangelize every person he met. He was passionate about reaching souls for Christ. He was inviting us to give our lives radically to God whatever it involved. As he gave that altar call, I almost ran forward. I felt so strongly that he was personally speaking right into my spirit. I received that call to give myself to Christ wholly.

About 1,500 people pressed towards the altar. There wasn`t enough room. People were lined up all up and down the aisles of the church. He was laying hands on some people and praying loudly into the microphone. I was receiving every word he spoke. I was yielding myself to God. I wish I could say he came and laid hands on me – but there were too many people. That doesn`t mean I didn't receive something. In fact, I believe that day I received a passion for the great commission. It was at that altar I received the baptism of the Holy Spirit as well – with no one laying hands on me. I received whatever God had for me, as much of God as God would give me. I received by faith in God. Never become religious and think, since there was no laying on of hands, nothing happened.

Discipleship and Mentoring

An example of where laying on of hands could be significant could be in a modern church someone is teaching a Bible class and gets an assistant to help him or her. The person trains the assistant so he or she knows what to do, how to do it etc. This exact thing occurred in my life. I was a recent convert, saved about one year. I had been in Bible class with a man nicknamed Skip and his wife, Polly. They instructed me, poured into me, loved me and were important in my life because I was the only Christian in my family. After the last Bible class was over, I wanted to say good bye but it was hard for me. As I started to speak about the end of the semester, Polly, spoke up and said: We want you to come to the next class. `I was relieved. I would still get to see them They had become spiritual parents to me. After the second class was complete, Polly approached me and asked me to stay on to help with the class. They got me to help take attendance, get materials, collect money, pray, lead in prayer etc. It was a learning experience because not only was I getting the Bible teaching but I was learning new ways of doing things and soaking up much of the passion for God both Skip and Polly had for God.

What happened is that I became a Bible teacher. I learned how to train others. I have had opportunity both to teach and also to train others for teaching. Imparting of an anointing or mentoring is not with every person you meet. You do it with someone you can spot the gifts in and or someone that God tugs at your heart to train. Not everyone can learn best from me. There is a chemistry between the mentor and the trainee. There is a smooth supernatural relationship where the person is trained and desires to learn all he or she can. You don`t do it casually. You do it prayerfully whether you are the mentor or the trainee. You believe it is God`s best and you give your best effort.

The Bible specifically warns us not to do it casually. It should be done with faith and prayerfully and for a specific purpose. Also, never let just anyone lay hands on you. Guard over this sacrament. Don`t regard it as casual. For example, there may be a class of 70 students; you may notice one or two individuals that have teaching gifts. It is those you should consider on training. It doesn`t mean you care less amount the others. It simply means you are to teach them but perhaps teaching isn`t their main gifting. Someone else should mentor them in some other area of gifting. The Holy Spirit will use us and speak to us about the individuals. The Holy Spirit will prompt us to invest in those individuals.

1 Timothy 5: 22 Do not lay hands suddenly on anyone, and do not partake of other men's sins. Keep yourself pure.

Also, you don't lay hands and pray for just anyone. As an altar prayer worker, I've had the opportunity to pray for hundreds of people who come to the altar for prayer. I would either hold the person's hand or touch the person on the shoulder or forehead. The people come forward for the purposes of prayer. It was done properly. Should I be mentoring someone, God will quicken to me what to do. My relationship with God is most important. I believe in divine associations. That is, God brings the people; God releases the gift; God instructs about the laying on of hands. It is all Holy Spirit lead. You should never just let anyone lay hands on you and you just never just lay hands on anyone. The reason is because there is an impartation and you don't just impart to anyone nor do you want just anyone imparting into your life.

Laying on of hands to impart a blessing

The laying on of hands was used by patriarchs in the Old Testament to pronounce generational inherited blessings over the children. In this passage. Jacob, who God called Israel, is praying a blessing on Joseph's sons Ephraim and Manasseh. He places his right hand on the youngest and his left hand on the oldest. This was not the way blessing were given. Usually the first born would be prayed for with the right hand on him. Joseph tries to correct Israel but Israel says it is God's choice not his own. He proclaims the larger blessing on the youngest one.

Genesis 48: 14 Israel stretched out his right hand and laid it on Ephraim's head, who was the younger, and his left hand on Manasseh's head, crossing his hands, for Manasseh was the firstborn.

15 He blessed Joseph and said,

"God, before whom my fathers
   Abraham and Isaac walked,
the God who fed me
   all my life long to this day,
16 the angel who redeemed me from all evil,
   bless the boys;

let them be called by my name,
 and the name of my fathers, Abraham and Isaac;
and let them grow into a multitude
 in the midst of the earth."

17 When Joseph saw that his father laid his right hand on the head of Ephraim, it displeased him, and he took hold of his father's hand to remove it from Ephraim's head to Manasseh's head. 18 Joseph said to his father, "Not so, my father, for this one is the firstborn. Put your right hand on his head."

19 His father refused and said, "I know it, my son, I know it. He will also become a people, and he will also be great, but truly his younger brother will be greater than he, and his descendants will become a multitude of nations." 20 He blessed them that day, saying,

"By you Israel will bless, saying,
 'May God make you like Ephraim and Manasseh.' "

So he set Ephraim before Manasseh.

Israel was about to die so he wanted to pass on the generational blessings of Abraham, Isaac and now Israel – to Joseph`s sons. It involved prayer and literal laying on of hands.

Laying on of Hands for Confirmation

The opportunity to lay hands on a person to confirm and ground the person in the truths he or she has studied is an essential part of our Christian faith. After studying the doctrines of Christ or after completing elementary teaching on Christian foundations, the students should receive confirmation. I don't know how much this is practiced in the protestant church but it should be.

After a nine-month study on the foundations of the Christian faith, we had a special part of the Church service where we went forward for confirmation prayer. The ministers laid their hands on us as we knelt and they prayed blessings upon us and that we would be firmly rooted in Christ. They prayed that our faith would be strong and that God would quicken the things we had been taught to us so we could live our lives for Christ.

We should pray for those who have completed foundational teaching and pray that the participants would be established in the faith. We should pray blessing over them. It not only shows that we approve of their studies but that we (ministers prayed but so did the congregation) receive them and strengthen them in the Christian faith. It is not simply a ritual. There were specific prayers over the different candidates. The person who prayed over me also prophesied over me. It was the leading of the Holy Spirit to establish me in the truths of Christ. They prayed for us to have a firm, strong foundation so we would only build on Christ as our foundation.

Healing

There are many occasions where the disciples laid hands on the sick and they were healed. It was not simply an outward action; it was an impartation of faith for healing. As Paul and his companions were ship wreaked, they came to an Island – it was Malta. Paul lays hands and prays for a person and he is healed.

Acts 28: 8 It happened that the father of Publius lay sick with a fever and dysentery. Paul visited him and, placing his hands on him, prayed and healed him. 9 When this happened, the rest on the island who had diseases also came and were healed.

Our churches should practice the laying on of hands for healing. Often, they will anoint with oil and pray for healing. Believing elders and ministry are often the ones who do it; sometimes altar prayer workers do it. We should offer this sacrament each week so that people who are in need of healing will be able to come. It should be preached from the pulpit regularly so people who are new or who are visiting can get the truth that Jesus Christ is the healer.

Hebrews 13: 8 Jesus Christ is the same yesterday, and today, and forever.

We should be teaching and practicing what the Word of God promises us. Jesus who died for our sins, also took upon Himself all the curses of the law from Deuteronomy 28. The Messiah would fulfill the promises of Isaiah. Jesus Christ is the Messiah.

Isaiah 53: 5 But he was wounded for our transgressions,
    he was bruised for our iniquities;
the chastisement of our peace was upon him,
    and by his stripes we are healed

The words "by his stripes we are healed" means salvation but also physical healing. The Apostle Peter uses these exact words to minister healing (2 Peter 2: 24). It is so important that we pray for one another so there will be no sick among us.

Some people believe the lie that God places sickness on a person to teach them or mature them. This is a direct lie that contradicts God 's words. Sickness was named as a curse of sin. God called it a curse. He most certainly would not use a curse to teach one of his children. The truth is some people have not read all of God's Word so if they hear a minister say such a thing as God is in it or some such language, they don't know there is healing. They don't know God.

Deuteronomy 28: 61 Also every sickness and every plague which is not written in the Book of the Law will the Lord bring upon you until you are destroyed.

The blessing of God is on those who serve God and honour Him. If that was true in the Mosaic covenant, it most certainly is true in the covenant of Jesus Christ who paid the full ransom for our lives with his life. Jesus helped show himself as Messiah by healing multitudes of people. If it was God's will to use sickness for those people, Jesus never would have healed them. The good news of the gospel of Jesus Christ means that you can be healed in spirit, soul and body.

Acts 10: 38 how God anointed Jesus of Nazareth with the Holy Spirit and with power, who went about doing good and healing all who were oppressed by the devil, for God was with Him.

Please notice God's Word says the sickness "oppressed by the devil" not a blessing of God.

In Matthew it states the following:

Matthew 12: 15 But when Jesus knew it, He withdrew from there. And great crowds followed Him, and He healed them all,

Since sickness is a curse not a blessing, people may foolishly believe that sickness is a direct result of sin. This is not true. Even the disciples believed that perhaps this was always true. Jesus corrects his disciples and heals the man and clearly says it was not because of sin and he showed God's will to heal.

John 9: 1As Jesus passed by, He saw a man blind from birth. 2 His disciples asked Him, "Rabbi, who sinned, this man or his parents, that he was born blind?"

3 Jesus answered, "Neither this man nor his parents sinned. But it happened so that the works of God might be displayed in him. 4 I must do the works of Him who sent Me while it is day. Night is coming when no one can work. 5 While I am in the world, I am the light of the world."

There are many excellent books on healing and receiving healing. If this is new information to you, please get yourself some Christian materials on healing. There are many present-day healing evangelists such as Oral Roberts, Gloria Copeland, Kenneth Copeland, Marilyn Hickey, Benny Hinn etc. I give you these names because all of them preach Jesus Christ the healer.

Healing comes through faith in Jesus Christ. Faith comes through the hearing of God's Word. It is essential for you to get scriptures about healing into your spirit. Get the scriptures into you by reading them out loud, hearing them and confessing them with your mouth. Reading the Bible and getting God's Word into you is essential for you to be proactive – get the scripture in you so that should something occur and sickness come, you can speak God's word over it and drive it out.

Results of the curse of sin

Sickness, disease, pestilence, hatred, wars, envy, strife – all these things are a result of the curse. Because Adam and Eve sinned, these things exist in our world. You may think God doesn't heal everyone. Please know that if a person is not healed – it is not God who choose to kill him or her. It is essential that we have faith in God's Word yes; it must be on the inside of our innermost being. It is also necessary for us to be wise stewards of our earthly bodies. Please note what we put in to our body directly effects our health.

The Body a Temple

In our modern North American Culture, we often dine on fast food – mostly greasy and salty and high in calories. A can of pop or soda is often 800 calories. A burger sometimes 1, 000. Calories. An average person should get 2, 500 – 3, 000 Calories a day. Junk food –lives up to its name. Chocolate bars, chips, candy – thousands of calories. Please do not pump these things into your body constantly and expect to be healthy. It matters what we put in. I don't pretend to be a dietician but I made some healthy food choices in my life several years ago because I want to live as long as I can.

1 Corinthians 6: 19 What? Do you not know that your body is the temple of the Holy Spirit, who is in you, whom you have received from God, and that you are not your own? 20 You were bought with a price. Therefore glorify God in your body and in your spirit, which are God's.

Through my explanation, please see that is God's desire for people to live long and be healthy. Also, each person must make wise healthy choices and teach his or her children etc. I have heard of, not witnessed, a miracle of weight loss. Someone overly obese who went for prayer because of all the health issues that arose because of obesity. Although the person was miraculously healed, the person went back to his or her poor habits and became ill once more.

Gloria Copland has an excellent book: Living Long: Finish Strong. It talks about this subject from a Christian point of view. Don't believe the lie that you have to die of a certain disease because it runs in your family. Don't believe the lie that you will die at an early age because others in your family did. Yes, we inherit some things from our families, but we can make a difference by doing our part both spiritually building up your faith and naturally by caring for our bodies.

Read the scriptures about healing. Do your part to be healthy but should there be sickness, most certainly get prayer for healing by someone with faith in Jesus the healer.

Matthew 18: 19 "Again I say to you, that if two of you agree on earth about anything they ask, it will be done for them by My Father who is in heaven. 20 For where two or three are assembled in My name, there I am in their midst."

Literally, as we pray for each other, Jesus Christ is in the midst of us and His presence can bring healing. The healing can be immediate or gradual. God also gifts doctors and health care professionals to use their skills to help save lives. I have received healing in all these ways. I give God the glory.

Immediate healing

I was not feeling well. I was ill. I believed I could not go to church. My friend came to pick me up as he usually did. I shared with him. He laid hands on me and prayed for me and I was immediately healed. I was able to go to church. It was instant.

Gradual Healing

I have been healed with gradual healing. I was very ill coughing etc. It was hard to breath etc. I read the scriptures to myself. I went to church knowing that they would pray for the sick. I went forward to a minister I knew believing in divine healing. She anointed me with oil and prayed a short prayer over me. I felt God's power go right through the top of my head. I don't know if I expected a longer more awesome prayer or what but as I walked I didn't notice any difference. I shared with my friends that I would have to go home because I wasn't well enough to go out. I believe they were both praying for me. They didn't say they were but I believe it. As I was on my way driving towards home, it suddenly dawned on me; I was breathing normally. I wasn't coughing. I felt excellent. I was healed. I shared it with them and we did our usual special Sunday dinner.

Anointing with oil

James 5: 14 Is anyone sick among you? Let him call for the elders of the church, and let them pray over him, anointing him with oil in the name of the Lord. 15 And the prayer of faith will save the sick, and the Lord will raise him up. And if he has committed any sins, he will be forgiven.

The Bible clearly instructs us what to do if we are ill. We should get elders or ministers to pray the prayer of faith over us for healing anointing us with oil. Oil is only a symbol of the Holy Spirit. There is no special magic about the oil. It is a symbol of God's presence. It reminds the person praying and the receiver to believe for the manifest healing presence of God.

This scripture covers various things. I want to discuss each of them so that your faith rises up for each of them.

1.   Call for the elders – if you cannot get to church, phone and ask someone to come pray for you. You must make a contact with somebody who can pray. You must realize God wants you healthy. Often, I have not only contacted my local church but ministries that I support because they pray and believe for healing.

2.   Anoint with oil in the name of the LORD – The LORD Jesus Christ – anointing with oil is what God commanded we do; we should obey. The oil is a symbol but God said to do it so we should do it.

3.   The prayer of faith will heal the sick. Usually the ill person needs a boost of faith by someone who is healthy and believes God's Word. It can be the person's own faith; it can be the faith of the minister. Faith must be present. You cannot pray unscriptural prayers like "If it be your will to heal O God…" and expect results. You will not find a prayer like it in the Bible anywhere. In Luke 5: 12 a leper says those words to Jesus and Jesus says I will heal you. Jesus heals him. A prayer of faith involves praying the scriptures over a person with true faith that impartation for healing is present.

4.   And if he has committed any sins – if the sickness comes because of sin or disobedience to God either neglecting your body or living outside of God's commandments – that is the realm of the curse. God promises, even if the person has sinned, he or she will be forgive as he or she comes for anointing with oil and the healing prayer of faith.

This specific points, should comfort any person because God has made provision in this sacrament that you might be healed: spirit, soul and body.

Healing in the soul of a person

Often people who have experienced the death of a loved one or a divorce or other such tragedy will be overcome with grief. It is normal to grieve the loss of a loved one but we as Christians do not grieve as the world grieves (1 Thessalonians 4: 13). The person who has become wounded in his or her spirit and is overcome with grief not only needs prayer but needs inner healing. Please know the lie that says that healing of such matters comes as years go by. Life may continue but healing doesn't naturally come to a deep wounded in the spirit. The soul of a person is the mind, will and emotions. It is at this level that grief comes. If you are strong in spirit, you can heal in soul. You will overcome the situation.

This is good news for anyone that came from a home where there was abuse or neglect or abuse or anything less than a Christian loving family. You don't have to remain a victim. You may have been abused physically, verbally or sexually. You do not have to remain a victim all your life. Do not be given over to self-absorption. If you focus on yourself and what was done to you and why it is unfair etc. you will stay a victim for the remainder of your life. I know this sounds like harsh words but if you know you are not happy with your life and you are thinking about how you were wounded or you can't see past the divorce or the death, you are in need of healing for your soul. Living in the realm of the soul is never the best for a Christian and it can lead to a wounded spirit.

Galatians 5: 16 I say then, walk in the Spirit, and you shall not fulfill the lust of the flesh.

Galatians 5: 25 If we live in the Spirit, let us also walk in the Spirit.

God wants us to live in the Spirit and constantly renew our strength in the Spirit. A broken spirit can occur when a person is constantly living in the soulish realm absorbed with what was done to him or her. This type of person cannot talk about anything without being negative. This type of person is like a black hole to anyone close to him or her. That is the person dumps negative stuff into the atmosphere around him or her. It is not a lack of compassion that causes me to say this. In fact, it is of understanding and compassion of God that compels me to say, no one has to live a victim of life. There is hope in Jesus Christ for healing of your soul.

Isaiah 53: 4 Surely he has borne our grief
    and carried our sorrows;
Yet we esteemed him stricken,
    smitten of God, and afflicted.
5 But he was wounded for our transgressions,
    he was bruised for our iniquities;
the chastisement of our peace was upon him,
    and by his stripes we are healed.

Mere positive thinking will not help a person wounded in the spirit. The person needs deep inner healing of the soul and possibly deliverance of an evil spirit of depression. The good news is that Jesus died for our sins and iniquities and our physical healing but also for our soul. He gave his life as a handsome for our souls. There is provision in the blood of Jesus and in the resurrected LORD for complete and total healing. Jesus took upon himself "the chastisement of our peace" that means he took the curse of all the negative stuff that could ever wound you or I and the curse of it died with Christ; Jesus rose from the dead in triumph over all things of the earth and the curse.

If this describes you or someone close to you, pray for the person yes, but the Word of God must be ministered to the person so he or she knows the truth of Jesus triumph.

John 8: 32 "You shall know the truth, and the truth shall set you free."

Romans 10: 17 So then faith comes by hearing, and hearing by the word of God.

The person should get faith teaching on the healing of the soul. Joyce Meyer has a strong testimony of complete and total healing and is a living example of this truth that Christ can take a broken person and completely heal and anoint and give new hope and life to a person. She has excellent books and teachings on beauty for ashes, and these topics. I highly recommend her CDs and books be shared with the person in need of inner healing. I have personally known of many people who were transformed by her testimony and her teachings. Once the person acknowledges he or she needs inner healing, the person should get prayer and anointing with oil from a minister of the gospel who believes that Jesus can heal the soul of a person.

I have experienced complete and total healing of my soul. I didn't even know what was going on. I didn't even know about my spiritual condition. I was a Christian, desiring to know God more. At first, I realized I had to come into agreement with God's Word and what God said about me. I started praying and confessing what God says about me. I began to notice my words more and more. The Holy Spirit was so gentle with me, leading me so that I could be transformed and know life beyond any joy I ever knew about. I prayed

Psalm 19: 14 Let the words of my mouth and the meditation of my heart
    be acceptable in Your sight, O Lord, my strength and my Redeemer.

Words we speak

I heard Gloria Copeland preach on God correcting us if we let Him. If we pray "Holy Spirit , please correct my mouth if my words do line up with your word." I prayed it and God started correcting me. If I said something dumb about myself or an insult, God checked me. Don't say negative things about yourself. You have to live with yourself always. Start saying I can do all things through Christ who strengthens me. Get the word "I can't" out of your vocabulary.

What we think about

What we think about matters. We can change how we feel depending on what we listen to or what we watch or what we hear. That is why it is so important to get teachings and scriptures to listen to. It is important to watch things that are pure. It is important to think about God's Word and what He says about us in His Word. For instance, God says we are more than conquerors in Christ Jesus. Guard your heart. Keep yourself wholly fixed on God and do not believe anything that goes against what God says in His Word.

Philippians 4: 8 Finally, brothers, whatever things are true, whatever things are honest, whatever things are just, whatever things are pure, whatever things are lovely, whatever things are of good report, if there is any virtue, and if there is any praise, think on these things.

Romans 8: 37 No, in all these things we are more than conquerors through Him who loved us.

Who we are with

Being with someone rather than alone is not always the answer to loneliness. A person who does not build you up spiritually and encourage you with scripture is not someone who can make a difference in your life positively. If the person is not encouraging you spiritually – be alone with God reading the scriptures, listening to them and saying them so your own ears can hear you speak them. What you say about yourself matters the most. If you can get your words in alignment with God's Word, you will start seeing a difference in your life. God will bring Christian friends in your life who will encourage you and strengthen and build you up. Until that occurs, keep constantly build up your own self with psalms and hymns and spiritual songs and scriptures (Ephesians 5: 19).

Jude 1: 20 But you, beloved, build yourselves up in your most holy faith. Pray in the Holy Spirit. 21 Keep yourselves in the love of God while you are waiting for the mercy of our Lord Jesus Christ, which leads to eternal life.

What we do

Give and it shall be given unto you (Luke 6: 38). I know it can mean finances but it can also be a principal of all of life in the Spirit. Start serving others. Start giving of yourself to care for others. If you can, get active in your local church by serving or baking at dinners. You could volunteer to start ministering with the Nursing Home Ministries, or teaching a Sunday school class. The principle of the kingdom of God is to give so that you may receive.

I knew of an elderly widow who not only attended all the churches prayer meetings to pray for others but also gave her home life to prayer and intercession for people, for the church for her family etc. If she got a word of God for you in prayer, it most certainly was something to cherish and pray about because she spent most of her life in prayer.

I remember how the more got involved in Church giving, the more I thought about others and less about myself. I saw people in nursing homes, who were dying and who received a bit of joy as I served communion to them or sang hymns with them. The more you serve others, the less you think about yourself.

Prayer for inner healing

The lie is that depressed people need to think about themselves. Just the opposite is true. Those people need to start caring for others. As they serve and give, God honours them by blessing them in so many ways, physically, financially and spiritually.

Receiving a prayer for inner healing is essential for those who have been wounded by life. It can occur with you and God privately. It can occur with a minister praying for you and anointing you with oil. In order to see a difference in your life, you must make a difference in your life. Start investing the Word of God into your life. Start serving and giving and pursuing God realizing the blessings that God has given to you and becoming thankful. Thank and praise God for what He has done for you. Focus on the blessings not on any negative thing. Focus on the Living Christ who lives in you. If you are living in the Spirit, you cannot live in the flesh. You cannot live in both. Choosing to honour God and to literally believe the Word of God and pray it and confess it and live it – is the answer that can bring a new life.

Jesus laid hands on the children imparting a blessing.

Jesus purposely imparted a blessing on children This was not a mere love for children or an outward sign. It was to impart a blessing. Children were not often considered important but Jesus showed their value by choosing them and using them as an example of simple, true faith.

Matthew 19: 13 Then little children were brought to Him that He might put His hands on them and pray. But the disciples rebuked them.

14 But Jesus said, "Let the little children come to Me, and do not forbid them. For to such belongs the kingdom of heaven." 15 He laid His hands on them and departed from there.

Mark 10: 15 Truly I say to you, whoever does not receive the kingdom of God as a little child shall not enter it." 16 And He took them up in His arms, put His hands on them, and blessed them.

If you are a parent, or have children in your life at all, pray for them. Pray God's blessing on them, protection as well as that they would come to live pleasing lives to God. I believe that parenting is an important responsibility and an awesome privilege because you have been entrusted to care for them; spiritually; you are the covering over the younger children until they can choose to live for Christ themselves.

My mother not only prayed for us as children but with her grandchildren, she would pray blessings over them each time she bathed them or they came to sit with her. It is a way of passing on a generational blessing of faith. It was especially important because I do not believe the parents prayed for their children. My mother prayed for them; I prayed for them and taught them Bible stories. I invested what I could into those who were in my life.

The Elders and Ministers

Part of what should be occurring in a Church service is that the elders and ministers should be laying hands on people who want a blessing. After I had first become a Christian, I went to every alter call for several years. I would pray about all thing in my life and give myself to God continuously. I have received many blessings by being quick to get prayer. I was the first Christian in my family so the prayers of those people were special to me. I had a Church family that prayed for me. Later, I became a prayer altar worker so that I could pray with others. I delighted in praying over people who came because I knew what God had done for me and believed He could also meet their needs.

Laying on of Hands for Ordination and Separation for Ministry

In Acts 13, Barnabus and Saul are separated for ministry together. The church prayed blessings and protection over them as they were sent out as missionaries. As a pastor or minister is dedicated to the service of God, Other ministers and elders lay hands on them separating them unto God for life long service. The person giving his or her life to serve God in ministry is giving wholly, spirit, soul and body to Jesus Christ for ministry. The ministers praying over them agree and often prophesies come forth because of the faith present.

Laying on of hands for Prophesy

1 Timothy 1: 18 This command I commit to you, my son Timothy, according to the prophecies that were previously given to you, that by them you might fight a good fight, 19 keeping faith and a good conscience, which some have rejected and suffered shipwreck in regard to their faith.

The Apostle Paul is reminding Timothy of the prophecies spoken over him. This type of friend is a treasure. A true godly friend will remind you of what God says about you and what prophecies you have received as promises of God. We should continuously remind God of what He has promised us, thanking Him for it and receiving it by faith even before we see a natural manifestation of it.

The gifts of the spirit can be released in a person by laying hands on that person and prophesying and praying in faith. There should be elders and pastors who flow in the prophetic. Apostles and Prophets are usually the ones who get the prophetic words over people but it could come from any of the five-fold ministry. Our part is to receive in faith and stir up the giftings with our prayers and with our words. We can receive callings on God on our life through the laying on of hands with prophesy. What occurs is that something that wasn't clear suddenly becomes clear and important as the known will of God for your life. Usually, it is a confirmation of something you already know about.

1 Timothy 4: 14 Do not neglect the gift that is in you, which was given to you by prophecy, with the laying on of hands by the elders.

Literally, write the prophecies for yourself and pray them. Say out loud "God I receive this calling…" Literally come into agreement with the prophetic word over your life so that you see it spiritually. Start thanking God for it. Ask the Holy Spirit to direct your steps, and lead you and bring godly doors of opportunity in your life so that you might fulfill the Word of God concerning your life.

Minister's Candidate school

After 3 years of studying for ministry, we were to receive the laying on of hands with prophesy. My pastor was a strong prophet of God who usually prayed over all the graduates and prophesied over them, In my particular class, he did not do it as usual. He delayed it for a year. He gathered together several known prophets of God who would all lay hands on us and prophesy over us. It was something I longed for. It was the culmination of my studies. It meant a blessing over my life. I fasted. Please know this is a big deal for me. Fasting and prayer should be a part of our Christian lifestyle, but it comes easier to some than others. I was so expectant of what God would say about me through the prophets. I was also nervous. I kept in prayer all the way to church and the service itself was charged with an atmosphere of faith for the prophetic. Gathering the prophets is a special atmosphere. If you have not experienced it, I highly recommend you get into a true prophet of God`s service. There is a special atmosphere for receiving miracles from God. I had studied three years of ministry classes, given myself to prayer and to serving in the Church. I wanted that special blessing that would come believing God would use those ministers to speak words of blessing over me.

In our graduating class, the ministers called each one of us up to the altar and we kneeled as the different prophets prayed and prophesied over us. They taped each person`s prophetic word so that we could remember and as proof so we could know what to pray for. I highly recommend that you get a tape or a CD of the personal prophecy as proof not only for your own self but as proof against any lie that may try to rise against it. I have kept those prophecies throughout the years and treasured them. I prayed them. I thank God for them. They have been like a compass to help me understand the seasons and help me to follow Christ.

Not just any person should lay hands on you. It should be somebody you respect, somebody you know, somebody who is true and sincere; the motives of the person`s heart matter. God will use prophets and apostles to prophesy and pray over those who believe to receive from the laying on of hands with prophesy. Faith is a key ingredient on your part and on the ministry team`s part.

Pray before you lay hands on someone

You should never lay hands on someone to impart a prophetic word unless you speak to God and God speaks to you or releases you to do so. If you are in part of a service where laying on of hands for prophesy is ministering, and you are in a position to lay hands, pray stirring up the gifts of God within you. Literally stir up the gift of faith; stir up the gift of prophecy; stir up the gift of words of wisdom; storr up the gift of word of knowledge; stir up the gift of discerning of spirits. As you do it, also pray that God would put the word of God in your mouth so that He would would glorified. It is serious and it should not be done lightly or without prayer.

If you are receiving the gift of prophecy with laying on of hands, pray before you are prayed for. Praise God; worship God – focus on Jesus Christ and on what He has done for you. Be in a position to receive. Stirr up the gift of discerning of spirits that you can agree with things of the Spirit of God and reject anything not of God.

Lay Hands on the Children in your life

Whether they are your own children, nieces or nephews   or grandchildren or neighbours, as the child sits with you pray a special prayer that the child will come to know Jesus as Saviour and live for God with his or her whole being. If they are infants, don't assume they don't understand you because they don't speak the language yet. Speak to them believing their spirits will receive a blessing. As the children are older, explain to them the simple truths of the gospel and should they desire, pray a salvation prayer with them. Pray for angels to guard over them. You have been given an opportunity to care for children, realize it is your chance to impart something spiritually as they are with you. The Apostle Paul yearned to be with people so he could impart gifts to them.

Romans 1: 11 For I long to see you, that I may impart to you some spiritual gift, so that you may be strengthened.

Lay Hands on your family

Should you be in a Christian family, no matter what the occasional, pray together at some point in your get together. Say a blessing over those in your family dinners etc. God may lead you to lay hands and pray over every member of your family. Obey these promptings. God has given you authority in the spheres of influence of your life – that includes praying for family.

You may be at church and God may prompt you to go pray for someone in the congregation or give an encouraging word. Usually, this occurs during the altar call, but it can occur at the usual greeting minutes where usually you just shake hands and greet people. Rather, you obey the promptings of the Holy Spirit. Never disrupt the service to do it.
1 Corinthians 14: 40 Let all things be done decently and in order.

Should you feel a prompting to pray for someone, do it discreetly. Either do it in a natural pause in the service or after the service. If God wants people to be released to pray for others, the pastor or presider of the meeting will get the prompting to do it.

Pray offering yourself to God so that he might impart a blessing to people as you gather with others. Expect God to use you. He will.

Romans 12: 1 I urge you therefore, brothers, by the mercies of God, that you present your bodies as a living sacrifice, holy, and acceptable to God, which is your reasonable service of worship.

7 RESURRECTION OF THE DEAD
AND ETERNAL JUDGEMENT

Chapter 7

Resurrection

Hebrews 6: 1 Therefore, leaving the elementary principles of the doctrine of Christ, let us go on to maturity, not laying again a foundation of repentance from dead works and of faith toward God, 2 of instruction about washings, the laying on of hands, the resurrection of the dead, and eternal judgment. 3 This we will do if God permits.

Resurrection

The Resurrection from the dead and eternal judgement are mentioned in the Old Testament as well as in the New Testament. There were two sects of Jewish believers while Christ was on the earth: The Sadducees and the Pharisees. The main difference about them is that the Pharisees interpreted the Old Testament scriptures believing in life after death or the resurrection. The resurrection is the belief in life after human life on earth. It is the teaching of the soul and spirit of a person returning to God.

A trace of mention of the afterlife through the covenants made with man

Death began with Adam's sin in the garden of Eden. God had warned Adam (and Eve was instructed because she was aware of it as she did it) that he could eat fruit from any of the trees in the garden of Eden except the Tree of the knowledge of Good and Evil.

Genesis 2: 17 but of the tree of the knowledge of good and evil you shall not eat, for in the day that you eat from it you will surely die."

Although Adam did not immediately physically die after eating the forbidden fruit, he was suddenly aware that he was naked and was ashamed. He had lost his covering of glory from God. Spiritually he feared God and tried to hide from Him. He died spiritually. His relationship with God was cut off. He could no longer enjoy God's friendship because he sinned against God. He lost his relationship with God. It was not only he and Eve, but it was all humans who would live after them. They sinned and brought judgement on all people who would live. Jesus Christ came as Messiah or Saviour to end the curse upon Adam; Jesus came to offer hope of eternal life and communion with God.

I do not believe it was God's design for Adam or Eve to ever die. If they had not sinned and possibly eaten from the Tree of Life instead, I believe all of human history would be completely different. I believe they would have lived forever and our lives would be as heaven on earth. There would have been no wars or murders or injustice or evil or sickness or death. The tree of life is an analogy for the LORD Jesus Christ.

God judged Adam with these words:

Genesis 3: until you return to the ground,
    because out of it you were taken;
for you are dust,
    and to dust you will return."

Adam and Eve were banished from the garden of Eden but they lived long lives and populated the earth. Adam lived 130 years (Genesis 5: 3). It was not until the birth of Enoch hundreds of years later that people started worshipping the LORD. I don't believe Enoch is mentioned only for his faith without any other reason. Again, hundreds of years passed and Noah is mentioned for his faith in God. God established a new covenant relationship with Noah. With Noah came hope of a new relationship for people with God.

With the Noahic Covenant God stated there would surely be an accountability for what a person did on earth. It is connected to the sin of murder. I interpret it to mean that a day of reckoning or a day of giving account for the things we have done in this life is certain.

Genesis 8: 5 But for your own lifeblood I will surely require a reckoning; from every animal will I require it; of man, too, will I require a reckoning for human life, of every man for that of his fellow man.

The next person God established covenant with is Abraham. Abraham was promised a multitude of descendants. He is acknowledged and respected because of his faith towards God. His death is recorded in the following way.

Genesis 25: 8 Then Abraham breathed his last and died at a good old age, an old man and full of years; and he was gathered to his people.

Abraham's Bosom

The term gathered with his people doesn't only refer to a burial site. There was a place the dead were gathered. It was known as Abraham's bosom. It was a place the believing righteous people went until the resurrection of Christ.

Moses

Most of Moses ministry was the promise of a future people who would follow the LORD and be blessed in the earth. God shows righteous judgement in all of the laws he gave to Moses for Israel. Once more the term gathered to your people is used by God speaking to Moses.

Deuteronomy 32: 50 Die on the mount where you go up, and be gathered to your people, just as Aaron, your brother, died on Mount Hor and was gathered to his people,

Isaiah

The prophet Isaiah is given prophetic vision for his generation and generations to follow. He foretells of the coming Messiah and gives many details that Jesus Christ fulfills. In this passage, the prophet is given a vision of the end of the age and judgement.

Isaiah 24: 21 In that day the Lord shall punish
    the host of heaven on high
    and the kings of the earth on the earth.
22 They shall be gathered together,
    as prisoners are gathered in the dungeon,
and shall be shut up in the prison,
    and after many days they shall be punished.

Isaiah 25: 9 It shall be said in that day:

Look, this is our God
    for whom we have waited that He might save us.
This is the Lord for whom we have waited;
    we will be glad and rejoice in His salvation.

The prophetic vision of a new heavens and earth is spoken by Isaiah also.

Isaiah 55: 17 For I create
   new heavens and a new earth;
the former things shall not be remembered
   or come to mind.

In the following verse judgement is proclaimed on a people. There future is prophesied. The mention of Sheol Hades is here as a place of the gathering of the unrighteous dead.

Ezekiel 26: 20 then I shall bring you down with those who descend into the pit, to the people of old, and make you dwell in the lower parts of the earth, in places desolate of old, with those who go down to the pit so that you will not be inhabited. But I shall set glory in the land of the living.

Ezekiel 31: For they all have been delivered to death, to the nether parts of the earth in the midst of the sons of men, with those who go down to the pit.

15 Thus says the Lord God: On the day when it went down to Sheol I caused mourning. I covered the deep over it and restrained its rivers, and its many waters were stayed. And I caused Lebanon to mourn for it, and all the trees of the field fainted for it.

Daniel

God gives the prophet Daniel a dream about the end of the age. It includes symbolic figures and beasts and creatures. Daniel fasts and prays about it because he does into know the meaning and earnestly seeks God concerning it. The angel Gabriel comes to him and gives him the interpretation of the dream. He mentions the following phrase which is certainly a reference to resurrection and judgement.

Daniel 12: 2 Many of those who sleep in the dust of the earth shall awake, some to everlasting life, but others to shame and everlasting contempt.

Ecclesiastes 3: 21 Who knows whether the spirit of man goes upward and the spirit of animals goes down to the earth?

Jesus teachings on Resurrection

Jesus preached it. His ministry on the earth was preaching salvation, healing and deliverance from sin and the joy of the resurrection.

John 5: 28 "Do not marvel at this. For the hour is coming in which all who are in the graves will hear His voice 29 and come out—those who have done good to the resurrection of life, and those who have done evil to the resurrection of judgment.

Resurrection and Judgement

Resurrection

Jesus clearly establishes the hope of the Resurrection as he is speaking with Martha and Mary because of the death of their brother Lazarus. Jesus reveals to her that He has authority over death. He does not say He can resurrect people. He says **He is** the Resurrection and the life. He is life. He is the essence of life. Later in the chapter, he demonstrates his victory over death by resurrecting Lazarus from the dead. Because he is the Messiah, Jesus who lived holy and died so that we might have eternal life – is the hope of the resurrection.

John 11: 24 Martha said to Him, "I know that he will rise again in the resurrection on the last day."

25 Jesus said to her, "I am the resurrection and the life. He who believes in Me, though he may die, yet shall he live. 26 And whoever lives and believes in Me shall never die. Do you believe this?"

27 She said to Him, "Yes, Lord, I believe that You are the Christ, the Son of God, who is to come into the world."

All people will live forever. People were created in the image of God: with a spirit, soul and body. The spirit and soul live forever. The human body dies because of the sin of Adam. There is a group of believers who will not know physical death. They will be transformed, changed in an instant. Their physical body will be changed. They will rise up into the air, be caught up to be with the LORD. God will gather the Christians from all over the earth.

1 Thessalonians 4: 16 For the Lord Himself will descend from heaven with a shout, with the voice of the archangel, and with the trumpet call of God. And the dead in Christ will rise first. 17 Then we who are alive and remain shall be caught up together with them in the clouds to meet the Lord in the air. And so we shall be forever with the Lord. 18 Therefore comfort one another with these words.

Your transformed Body

We don't know much about the transformed bodies we will get but from Jesus example we can learn several things. Jesus was able to pass through a locked chamber. Jesus appeared. He had his physical body. They recognized him as Jesus. They saw the wounds in his hands and feet. They knew it was Jesus.

John 20: 19 On the evening of that first day of the week, the doors being locked where the disciples were assembled, for fear of the Jews, Jesus came and stood in their midst, and said to them, "Peace be with you." 20 When He had said this, He showed them His hands and His side. The disciples were then glad when they saw the Lord.

They were able to dine with Jesus. He was not merely a spirit. He had a type of resurrected body that was more than human but not simply spirit. He appeared on the earth to people for forty days. He appeared to the disciples and had dinner with them.

Luke 24: 39 See My hands and My feet, that it is I Myself. Feel Me and see. For a spirit does not have flesh and bones as you see that I have."

John 21: 12 Jesus said to them, "Come and eat breakfast." None of the disciples dared ask, "Who are You?" They knew it was the Lord. 13 Jesus came and took the bread and gave it to them, and likewise the fish.

The Resurrection

The book of Revelation describes the Resurrection because both resurrection and Judgement are discussed in it.

The Scriptures teach of two separate judgements: a judgement Throne of Jesus Christ and the

The Judgement Seat of Jesus Christ

Jesus who conquered sin, hell and the grave, has been exalted to the highest place. He is seated right next to God. He will judge all of the Christians and believers who came to Christ while he was in Abraham's Bosom – so that would be all believers in Jehovah. It is a glorious day for those of us who revere and honour God but also it is the ending of hope for those who did not give their lives to Jesus Christ.

A day is coming, when there will be no more preaching of salvation. The preaching of salvation is the main purpose for the Christian Church on earth. After the Christian Church (universal – all believers) is caught up to be with God, there will be people on earth who realize they missed the rapture. They will immediately turn to Jesus Christ and repent knowing it was preached to them. There are others who will also come to Christ. But on the day of the Judgement Seat of Christ, there will be no other salvations after it. The scripture tells those who are resurrected in the first resurrection to rejoice because the judge is also the person who paid the penalty for all sin – Jesus Christ. He will judge us by how we lived our lives as Christians. We will be judged as believers.

Revelation 20: 4 I saw thrones, and they sat on them, and the authority to judge was given to them. And I saw the souls of those who had been beheaded for their witness of Jesus and for the word of God. They had not worshipped the beast or his image, and had not received his mark on their foreheads or on their hands. They came to life and reigned with Christ for a thousand years. 5 The rest of the dead did not come to life until the thousand years were ended. This is the first resurrection. 6 Blessed and holy is he who takes part in the first resurrection. Over these the second death has no power, but they shall be priests of God and of Christ and shall reign with Him a thousand years.

White Throne judgement.

The White Throne Judgement is the second Judgement; it is of non-believers. They will be judged by the laws of Moses. They will be judged how they lived their lives. They will be sentenced to eternal punishment. They will be judged for not accepting Jesus as the sacrifice for their sins.

Revelation 20: 11 Then I saw a great white throne and Him who was seated on it. From His face the earth and the heavens fled away, and no place was found for them. 12 And I saw the dead, small and great, standing before God. Books were opened. Then another book was opened, which is the Book of Life. The dead were judged according to their works as recorded in the books. 13 The sea gave up the dead who were in it, and Death and Hades delivered up the dead who were in them. And they were judged, each one by his works. 14 Then Death and Hades were cast into the lake of fire. This is the second death. 15 Anyone whose name was not found written in the Book of Life was cast into the lake of fire.

What is important here is that God keeps records of what people do on earth. God knows all things. The scripture says God keeps books. Finally, those in Sheol Hades in the center of the earth will be judged. They were the unrighteous people. The punishment is eternal torment with the devil and the demons.

The Final Judgement

There have been sort of non-scriptural interpretations of hell as a place where the devil torments people. That is completely unscriptural. The devil will be in torment himself. There is separation from God; God is joy, life, peace, love, mercy, kindness, etc. The fruit of the spirit describes God's character.

Galatians 5: 22 But the fruit of the Spirit is love, joy, peace, patience, gentleness, goodness, faith, 23 meekness, and self-control; against such there is no law. 24 Those who are Christ's have crucified the flesh with its passions and lusts. 25 If we live in the Spirit, let us also walk in the Spirit. 26 Let us not be conceited, provoking one another and envying one another.

God is merciful. He has shown so much mercy and given people so many chances to come to know him. It is evident in his relationship with Israel. It is evident in His mercy towards Christians on the Earth. It is by God's command that our Earth exists. It is by God's creativity that people can achieve and build and learn. It is by God's reaching out towards people throughout the thousands of years that people have had opportunities to know God. The absence of God would be the most horrible thing beyond what a person could conceive of.

The Life to Come for Believers

A new heavens and a new earth is to come. Man has not been a wise steward with so much of the earth and the atmosphere of it. Because of our sin, the earth was cursed. Also, there will be many judgements poured out on the earth during the outpouring of judgements on the nations. It will include the destruction of earth and water as well as people. God Himself promises to live in the midst of the New Jerusalem and to rule with us on the new earth. It is in the new kingdom there will be no sin and no sorrow. There will only be joy and pleasures beyond what a human can imagine. God is fascinating. God is magnificent. Many people will want to simply worship and praise with all the angels.

God who gave us intellect, creativity, imagination, insight, wisdom, skills, gifts, talents will not give us less in the resurrection. Truly His brilliance and character will be revealed to us throughout eternity. A revelation of God will occur; one moment after, new revelation of God will occur. It is like eternal joy springing up forever. The language used describes eternal life in human terms. The most awesome aspects of human life are only an entrance for us to understand the joy that is to come. God will live with us. The life that Adam and Eve could have partaken of the Tree of Life in the garden of Eden will be the only life we will know.

Revelation 21: 21 Then I saw "a new heaven and a new earth."[a] For the first heaven and the first earth had passed away, and there was no more sea. 2 I, John, saw the Holy City, the New Jerusalem, coming down out of heaven from God, prepared as a bride adorned for her husband. 3 And I heard a loud voice from heaven, saying, "Look! The tabernacle of God is with men, and He will dwell with them. They shall be His people, and God Himself will be with them and be their God. 4 'God shall wipe away all tears from their eyes. There shall be no more death.'[b] Neither shall there be any more sorrow nor crying nor pain, for the former things have passed away."

Revelation 22: 1 Then he showed me a pure river of the water of life, clear as crystal, flowing from the throne of God and of the Lamb 2 in the middle of its street. On each side of the river was the tree of life, which bore twelve kinds of fruit, yielding its fruit each month. The leaves of the tree were for the healing of the nations. 3 There shall be no more curse. The throne of God and of the Lamb shall be in it, and His servants shall serve Him. 4 They shall see His face, and His name shall be on their foreheads. 5 Night shall be no more. They need no lamp nor the light of the sun, for the Lord God will give them light. And they shall reign forever and ever.

Our hope as believers is in Jesus Christ and in eternal life. Although there will be a new heavens and a new earth, we will always with be God who will living with us in joy that is beyond all human expression.

CONCLUSION

Conclusion

To Christians, the teachings in this book will either confirm truths they have been taught or reveal some teachings that perhaps they only knew in part. The book is used to teach the basic doctrine of the Christian faith, They are the main doctrines of Christ that the apostles preached and that The Apostle Paul taught. Also, these doctrines are found in some aspect in all the Christian churches.

To a new Christian, perhaps some of these things are new to you. You should get into a Christian Church where you can learn these things. Talk with other believers about them. Read the Bible yourself. Get a version that you can understand. My favourite version is the King James Version but it is not used by many churches today.

I have used scripture in this book from the Modern English Version which is an interpretation of the King James preserving the meaning. The New Living edition is very easy to read. The message Bible is in ordinary even slang language. Get a version that you can understand. Read it and pray asking God to give you revelation. It is essential that you get into a church where you can learn more about God and develop godly friendships.

It is my hope that by reviewing the foundations of the doctrines of Christ, you will be stronger in your Christian faith and perhaps some scripture will be quickened to you that it would give you hope and encouragement.

Hebrews 6: 1 Therefore, leaving the elementary principles of the doctrine of Christ, let us go on to maturity, not laying again a foundation of repentance from dead works and of faith toward God, 2 of instruction about washings, the laying on of hands, the resurrection of the dead, and eternal judgment. 3 This we will do if God permits.

.

PRAYERS

The following prayers are samples of prayers you could pray for important reasons. You could pray the same meaning in your own words. The prayers are meant as examples only.

PRAYER FOR SALVATION

Thank you- Jesus that you died for me on the cross. Thank you that you rose from the dead and ascended into heaven. Thank you that you are coming back again. I thank you Jesus for forgiving my sins. Thank you for your blood that cleanses me from all sin and unrighteousness. Thank you that your blood makes me holy. Thank you for saving me. Fill me with the Holy Spirit to overflowing. I pray for the baptism of the Holy Spirit. Lead me to other people who love you and serve you and that can help me know more about you. Give me the discerning of spirits strong. I thank you and praise you. With my mouth, I confess Jesus Christ is my LORD. Amen.

PRAYER FOR BAPTISM OF THE HOLY SPIRIT

Thank you- Jesus that you promised to send the gift of the Holy Spirit to us. Thank you that this promise is to all believers. I am a believer. I want all of you that you will give me. I want to know you God. Baptize me in the Holy Spirit with the evidence of speaking in other tongues. I believe you want to fill me to overflowing with your Spirit so that I might be an effective witness for Christ on the earth. Thank you for saving me. Thank you for your Holy presence. [begin praising God for what He has done for you – sing worship choruses and praise God in your natural language. Believe that He is present with you – start praising and worshipping Him. As phrases come to you in other tongues, say them – praise God with new tongues.] I praise you. I thank you. I receive the baptism of the Holy Spirit.

PRAYER FOR RELEASING ANGELS

God, I thank you that angels are ministering spirits sent as ministers to us. I pray over my prayer request NAME IT HERE. God I pray release angels to perform it. I thank you for releasing the answer to me. I praise you for it. Amen.

PRAYER FOR RESISTING EVIL

I am the redeemed of the LORD. Jesus Christ has saved me. I am a new creation in Christ Jesus. Jesus blood covers me. I live in the spirit. The Holy Spirit of God fills my spirit. O Holy Spirit quicken me; give me wisdom. Pray [expecting God will give you discerning of spirits so you will have the right words to speak.]

In the name of Jesus Christ, I bind you. I rebuke you evil spirit. In the name of Jesus, I command you to go out. You have no place in my life. I cast you out. You have no place with me. I am covered by the blood of Jesus and His righteousness is my righteousness. Go out evil spirit in the name of Jesus Christ!
Thank you, Holy spirit for your holy presence. Release angels to drive out the enemy. Thank you. Amen.

PRAYER FOR PROTECTION

Holy Spirit release angels to protect me. I plead the blood of Jesus over me. I pray the protection you promise to your people. Cover me Jesus. Holy Spirit give me wisdom, discernment and understanding. Thank you for angels that guard over me. Thank you for your blood that protects me and a hedge of protection around me. I praise you O God. [praise God with some worship choruses and expect God's holy presence to be manifest in you]. Thank you. O God for protection. Amen.

OTHER BOOKS BY CHRIS A. LEGEBOW

Available on Amazon.ca Amazon.com or Amazon.ca or Kindle
Or the Create Space webstore.

Living Word Publishers

Angels: Ministering Spirits

An Excellent Spirit: Living Life Wholly Unto God

Covenant With God: God's Relationship With Man

Discovering and Using your Spiritual Gifts

The Doctrine of Christ: Essential Truths of Scripture

The Five-Fold Ministry: Gifts to the Church

Kinds of Prayer. Knowing Them and Using Them Effectively

Living Life Fully: Knowing your Purpose

The Anointing: the Glory of God

The High Calling: Life Worth Living

The Sacraments: A Charismatic Guide

ABOUT THE AUTHOR

Chris Legebow is a Christian Professor of English and Communications. She has taught at the elementary, high school and College and University levels. She has ministered in her local churches in intercessory prayer, teaching Sunday school and other Christian Doctrine classes to children and youths. She has preached to congregations and given her testimony. Although she was not raised in a Christian home, she came to know Jesus Christ as her Saviour and LORD while she was studying in University. This radically transformed her life in terms of priorities and commitment. She has a strong passion for the great commission – that Jesus Christ would be preached throughout all the earth believing that it a major sign of the LORD's return. She has been a part of several different types of full gospel charismatic churches but has also gained much of her insight and enlightenment from Christian Media and broadcasting. She hopes to continue ministering, serving, interceding and giving and teaching until the LORD returns.

www.ingramcontent.com/pod-product-compliance
Lightning Source LLC
Chambersburg PA
CBHW021202020426
42331CB00003B/167